Deadly Days
in
Kansas

DEADLY DAYS IN KANSAS

by
Wayne C. Lee

The CAXTON PRINTERS, Ltd.
Caldwell, Idaho
1997

Library of Congress Cataloging-in-Publication Data

Lee, Wayne C.

Deadly Days in Kansas / by Wayne C. Lee.
p.   cm.
Includes bibliographical references and index.
ISBN 0-87004-379-x

1. Frontier and pioneer life – Kansas – Anecdotes. 2. City and
town life – Kansas – History – 19th century – Anecdotes. 3.
Violence – Kansas – History – 19th century – Anecdotes. 4. Kansas
– History – Local – Anecdotes.   I. Title.
F685.L44   1997   97 – 18894
978.1'03-dc21   CIP

Printed, lithographed and bound in the United States of America by
The CAXTON PRINTERS, Ltd.
Caldwell, Idaho 83605
162715

CONTENTS

ILLUSTRATIONS

PREFACE

To the Indians, the Great Plains was a vast buffalo pasture. The heart of that pasture was what the white man chose to call Kansas. For centuries, the Indians claimed the region as their larder. They harvested most of the necessities of life from the huge buffalo herds and never depleted the supply.

Then the whites came – first in cautious dribbles, then like a flood breaking over a dam. They poured into the big pasture and began destroying the Indians' storehouse. They wanted to get rid of the great herds of buffalo, plow up the buffalo grass, and change the great pasture into what they called civilization. That meant starvation for the Indians. They fought back.

But that was only one part of the change. The white men fought each other for a larger parcel of that great pasture. They even had a great war among themselves to decide how they would govern their land. While the western half of the Kansas Territory was a battlefield between white and red men, the eastern part was a different kind of war.

In the west, greedy men tried to claim the lion's share of the new wealth they had found. And some, with no scruples at all, tried to steal what the others had worked so hard to claim.

The farmers and merchants followed the retreat of the Indians and they laid out towns, built churches, established schools. But it was the greedy, the callous, the unscrupulous, who turned some of those well-planned, peaceful towns into deadly towns. Law took the shape of a six-gun or a shotgun. Order was restored in gunsmoke and, more often than not, was followed by funerals.

They say that behind every new home there is a lifetime of dreams, hopes, and hard work. Behind almost every peaceful Kansas town of today, there is a turbulent history, sometimes violence, often killings, as law and order fought its way to dominance.

This book details a few of the many battles fought to bring law and order during those deadly days in Kansas.

I
1840 — 1859

Bleeding Kansas

Buried Treasure on the Trail
Rice County — 1843

Kansas Territory hadn't been established in 1843. The Republic of Texas claimed part of what would become southwestern Kansas.

Who claimed the area was of little importance to Jose Chaves. He was intent on getting his two wagons to Independence, Missouri, each well filled with hides he had collected in Santa Fe. In St. Louis, he could sell them to pay for the trip, then buy loads of merchandise to take back to Santa Fe and reap a healthy profit. He had a fortune in gold and coins to pay for that merchandise.

Everything was going well for him until a late winter storm hit the caravan a short time after it passed the big bend in the Arkansas River. It turned bitter cold. Chaves had about fifty mules with him, some possibly for barter, but most to help haul back the heavy loads he planned to bring. The storm was so severe that most of the mules died and the five men with Chaves almost did the same.

When the storm was over, they found only five mules still alive, not enough to pull the two loaded wagons. Chaves had no choice but to wait, hoping a train would

come by and he could buy enough animals to continue his journey eastward.

But it wasn't another train that showed up. It was fifteen men on horseback from Missouri who fit the description of a group known as Missouri Ruffians. The leader of the Missouri riders was a man named John McDaniel. He claimed to be aligned with Texas in the dispute between Texas and Mexico. That dispute would soon erupt into war.

Seeing that Chaves' group were all Mexican, McDaniel took them prisoner. Then he methodically robbed each traveler of everything of value. Chaves was a cautious man. Knowing there were men like McDaniel along the trail, he had buried his money until he was able to go on to Missouri.

Most of McDaniel's men thought they had taken everything they could get and were ready to go back to Missouri. They took the five mules that were still alive as part of their share of the booty, put the loot on the mules, and headed back east.

McDaniel, however, was certain that Chaves had a lot of money hidden somewhere. He was obviously going after loads of merchandise to take back to Santa Fe. He'd have to pay for it in cash. Where was the

Early day
Lawrence, Kansas.

Kansas State Historical Society

money? McDaniel and the men still with him beat Chaves, trying to make him tell where he had hidden the money. Chaves was stubborn. He wouldn't tell. If he didn't take his loads of merchandise back to Santa Fe, he might as well be dead.

McDaniel tried for a day to beat the secret out of Chaves but he wouldn't talk. Finally, in desperation, McDaniel stood Chaves by the river and brought his five men out to stand in front of him. He killed the Mexican helpers, one-by-one. But still Chaves would not reveal where the money was hidden. Finally, McDaniel dragged Chaves to the bank of the river and gave him one last chance to tell where he had hidden the money. Chaves refused. McDaniel shot him.

The bodies were loaded into a wagon and pushed it into the creek. Then the raiders rode back to Missouri.

Somehow the story of what had happened to Jose Chaves reached Missouri. Perhaps one of McDaniel's men made a slip of the tongue. McDaniel was arrested and tried for the murder of Chaves. During the

trial, McDaniel told about the money he was still sure Chaves had buried somewhere. The legend of the buried treasure was born and survived for many years.

First Sack of Lawrence Douglas County — 1856

The Missouri Compromise was supposed to solve the problems in Missouri and Kansas concerning the slavery question. But in 1854, the Kansas-Nebraska Act repealed the Missouri Compromise and set new rules. Kansas would hold elections as soon as there were enough settlers, and they would vote to be either pro-slavery or slave free. On paper, that looked like the democratic thing to do. But the question wasn't going to be settled on paper. The Free-Staters rushed in as many people from the northern states as they could. The pro-slavery element poured Missourians across the border.

The eastern part of Kansas was being settled rapidly but not amiably. The Free-

Staters set up their headquarters in Lawrence, while the Pro-Slavery group settled wherever they felt they could have the most influence. Some people could be frightened out of voting and neither side was above using any tactic that would guarantee success.

Serious trouble threatened at every turn. The lid popped off when Charles Dow, a Free-Stater, was murdered by Franklin Coleman, a pro-slavery man. Coleman fled to Shawnee and in the process of settling the question, another Free-Stater, Jacob Branson, was arrested by Sheriff Sam Jones. But he was spirited away by friends and Jones swore vengeance.

Jones called for the militia and it came from Missouri, which didn't calm the Free-Staters' nerves. Calm was restored momentarily but the underlying current remained.

There could have been more trouble that winter if the weather had not been so bad. Snow and cold put a damper on tempers and most people stayed at home.

The election came during the winter and Missourians packed the ballot boxes, coming up with a pro-slavery government. The Free-Staters called it a bogus government and held an election of their own. Charles Robinson was elected governor on the Free-State ticket and he took over.

Spring arrived. With it came a flood of Bibles from Henry Ward Beecher. Beecher supported the Free-Staters and the pro-slavery group insisted that Beecher was shipping rifles in boxes marked "Bibles".

The pro-slavery men got warrants sworn out for certain Free-Staters in Lawrence but when the deputy-marshal went there to make the arrests, he was turned away. This caused Sheriff Sam Jones to call for aid. It was Missourians who rushed in to help and they marched on Lawrence. When they got there, the Free-Staters allowed the deputy-

marshal to make his arrests and the situation was declared settled.

But they hadn't reckoned on Sheriff Jones. He assumed command of the men who had come to back up the deputy-marshal making the arrests. Jones led the men into Lawrence and sacked the town.

They destroyed the hotel, the newspaper office, and Governor Robinson's house. It was the most complete destruction that had taken place up to that point in the conflict between the Free-Staters and the pro-slavery elements.

It backfired on the pro-slavery group because many people felt the raid was entirely uncalled for. The Free-Staters formed guerrilla bands and roamed the country-side looking for pro-slavery men. It promised little peace for Kansas.

Pottawatomie Massacre
Pottawatomie County — 1856

John Brown had a reputation for being a little off balance mentally before he came to Kansas. He was also known for his extreme hatred of slavery and the men who promoted it. Five of his sons came to Kansas during the turmoil. He followed them in time to express his fury at the destruction in Lawrence at the hands of Sheriff Jones and his men.

The climate was right for any man who wanted to take an active role in gathering men of like thinking and heading up a small army. Sometimes it was only a half dozen men. Other times it could be a hundred. John Brown had five sons who were willing to follow him and that gave him a good start on a reckless company of troublemakers.

The destruction of the hotel, newspaper office and Governor Robinson's house in Lawrence was the match that lit John Brown's fuse. He didn't go after Sheriff

Jones and his men. Instead, he went up into Pottawatomie County where there was a settlement of belligerent pro-slavery supporters.

Brown led his little army along Pottawatomie Creek and struck target. He made no big show of being there and there was no battle. But the next day, neighbors found the dead mutilated bodies of five men. The mutilation would have done credit to an Indian massacre.

It didn't take long to identify who had committed the crimes. But, except for the mutilation, it was no worse than some of the other battles that had been fought. But it added to the legend of John Brown's ferocious hatred of slavery and its proponents.

This massacre was another little lightning strike, the kind that would eventually set the entire prairie ablaze. A Captain Pate went after Brown to capture him and bring him to justice. Pate not only failed, but he and his men were taken prisoner by Brown and his followers. They were held for a while before being released. The incident occurred well to the south, below Lawrence, near the southern border of Douglas County.

John Brown remained free, still thinking of other fields where his fury could strike a telling blow. The new state continued to earn its reputation of "Bleeding Kansas."

Starvation Trail
Logan, Sherman Counties — 1859

The Blue brothers of Illinois, Alexander, Daniel and Charles, heard of the gold strike in the foothills of the mountains in what was then the western edge of Kansas. Sure that one season in the gold fields would put them on Easy Street for the rest of their lives, they headed west in late winter.

Leaving the Missouri River on foot with only a pack horse, since they didn't have money enough for saddle horses, the brothers headed west in early March. They had several companions, also on foot.

Most of the travelers, short of supplies, had to stop to hunt game along the Smoky Hill River. The Blue brothers, certain they had plenty of food to get them to the gold fields, pressed on with one companion, George Soley.

From that day on, misfortune and tragedy stalked the men. Indians stole their pack horse. They packed as many supplies as they could carry on their backs and went on.

They made a bad decision at the junction of the Smoky Hill and the Republican Rivers. They chose the Smoky Hill route because it was shorter. But they didn't know it didn't have water all the way. They made another bad decision when they didn't stop to kill game. They were sure there would be plenty of game to be had all along the trail. They were wrong.

Their third bad decision came at the forks of the Smoky Hill River. The North Fork appeared to have a bigger trickle of water than the South Fork so they went on the North Fork. But it was the South Fork that carried the most water. A few miles up the North Fork, the water disappeared.

They ran out of food. There was no game. They had to dig deeper and deeper into the riverbed to find water and finally they found nothing but dry sand.

Alexander got sick. Knowing his chances of survival were slim, he told the others that, if he died, they were to eat his body. It was their only hope. They refused the idea.

Another bad storm stopped them from moving. When it was over, it was Soley, not Alexander, who was the first to die. The brothers balked at eating human flesh but finally they did. Survival is the primary instinct of every animal, including man.

Alexander died next. His brothers rebelled at the thought of eating his flesh. But self preservation triumphed and Daniel and Charles lived a few more days.

Then Charles died. Daniel had been the strongest of the brothers from the first. But now he simply lay down beside his brother to die, too.

But three Arapaho Indians found Daniel and took him to their camp. He was nourished back to health, taken to the stage line and sent on into Denver.

Daniel's interest in searching for gold crumbled into the dust of tragedy. He took the stage back east where he wrote the story of the fatal trip.

NOTE: For details of this trip, see the booklet, Thrilling Narrative of the Adventures, Sufferings and Starvation of Pike's Peak Gold Seekers on the Plains of the West in the Winter and Spring of 1859, by Daniel Blue, published by the Evening Journal Steam Press of Chicago in 1860; or Trails of the Smoky Hill by Wayne C. Lee & Howard C. Raynesford, pp 39-41, published by The Caxton Printers, Ltd., 1980.

The Doy Rescue
Doniphan County — 1859

When the Kansas-Nebraska Bill became law in 1854, it opened the gates to a mighty struggle in Kansas between Free-Staters and the pro-slavery settlers. Congress, in all its wisdom, decreed that the vote of the settlers would determine whether Kansas would be a free state or a slave state. But it made no provision for controlling the situation until that vote was taken. Both the pro-slavery and the free state leaders recognized the absolute

necessity of getting their own settlers into the area first.

The Emigrant Aid Society was organized in Boston by Free-Staters The society sent men west to direct the settlement drive. Those men picked up Doctor John Doy on their way to Kansas Territory. They settled in Lawrence. Slaves who escaped from their masters headed for Kansas, knowing that they would get help if they could get to Lawrence.

During the winter of 1858-1859, several escaped slaves reached Lawrence. Instead of forwarding them one at a time, the Emigrant Aid Society decided to wait until they had several, then send them in a large group. Doctor Doy was chosen to handle the chore. They got two covered wagons to carry the slaves under loads of legitimate freight. A collection was taken up from Free-Staters to buy blankets and provisions for the escapees on their trip.

Doctor Doy started out with his two wagons of cargo but didn't get far before he was stopped by a bandit gang of Missourians. It was the one fear they all had in making the trip. They learned later that a man who had contributed a small amount to the collection was a spy who got word to the bandits where and when the wagons would be traveling.

The two wagons and their cargo were taken to Missouri. Doctor Doy was turned over to authorities while the slaves were disposed of. Likely, they were sent south and sold into slavery again. It was a lucrative business for the bandits.

Doctor Doy was charged with kidnapping slaves and was sentenced to five years in the penitentiary. He appealed his case. He was held in the St. Joseph jail until his appeal was heard.

The Free-Staters were furious. If Doy had committed any crime, it had been in Kansas where Missouri had no jurisdiction.

They had taken him into Missouri illegally. And no one could convince a Free-Stater that Doy had committed any crime. They formed a committee to free Doy.

It took the group some time to devise a plan that had any chance of success. Spies told them where Doy was being held. Getting their men over into St. Joseph was easy. Getting Doy out of the jail would be a problem. Getting him back across the river into Kansas would be an even bigger problem. They'd have to do it very stealthily or they could all get killed.

Ten men were assigned to the committee. All were dedicated to freeing Doy. None of them was more determined than Charles Doy, Doctor Doy's son. They made a spying trip across the river, taking the ferry both ways. That aroused no suspicions. They found the jail on the border of the town square. They stayed in the square until they discovered which cell Doy was in. Then they walked the streets until they decided on the best escape route. They'd have to have a boat because they couldn't take the ferry back. They located the spot where some fishermen tied up their boats and also found where they hid their oars. With the necessary information in hand, they set the date for the adventure.

The conspirators took a wagon and team down to the river and left them close to the spot where they hoped to land with Doy. Then the ten men caught the ferry across the river to the Missouri side. There they spread out, each man appearing to be on a different mission.

There was heavy traffic back and forth across the river. The gold strike along the foot of the Rocky Mountains had put many men on the go. So a teamster on his way to pick up a load of lumber; a man looking for a lot to buy to build a store, and a farmer in town for some repairs, didn't stir any suspicion.

The farmer, Joseph Gardner, went to the town square, got a drink, then took off his shoes and soaked his feet in a watering trough. While he sat there, he made hand signals to Doctor Doy looking from his cell window.

Late that evening, one of the ten, dressed like a traveler, appeared at the jail door and asked to see Doy. He said he had a message to deliver to him from his family. The jailer let him in and he talked to the prisoner. Then, diverting the jailer's attention, the messenger backed against the cell door and pressed a note into Doy's hand. The note advised the doctor to be ready at midnight.

The plan was moving along on schedule. About nine o'clock, a heavy rain hit the town. That didn't change any plans. In fact, it worked in favor of the schemers. It drove most people off the streets.

About one o'clock, the conspirators put their most important step into action. Three of the ten committee members showed up at the jail. One appeared to be a Kansas sheriff, one his deputy, and the other their prisoner with his hands tied securely. They roused the jailer and told him that the jail in Hiawatha, Kansas, had burned and they needed a place to put the prisoner.

The jailer, roused out of his sleep, was not too gracious. But he allowed the visiting sheriff to lock his prisoner in the jail temporarily. He led the party to the cells and unlocked a door. The prisoner objected to going into the cell. While the jailer was trying to convince the prisoner to come in, he suddenly found himself between a gun on one side and a large knife on the other.

One man demanded to know if John Doy was in the jail. Doy himself answered, appearing dressed for travel with his few belongings in his hand. They untied the "prisoner" and stepped outside the cell, threatening the jailer with death if he made any noise for half an hour. One man faked staying in the front of the jail and the jailer, locked in the cell, kept quiet.

The rain was still falling and it gave members of the party a good excuse for covering their faces as they walked toward the spot where the boats were tied up. They did find a couple of policemen on the street but the officers paid little attention to them while trying to keep the rain out of their own eyes.

The boats they chose leaked and one man in each boat had to bail as they crossed the river. But they made it. The rescue had come off without a hitch.

A footnote to the story reveals how the Free-Staters discovered who had tipped off the Missourians that Doy was taking the slaves north. By checking out each contributor, they pinpointed the pro-slavery man. He was called before a meeting held in Lawrence, Shalor Eldridge, presiding. The general sentiment was to hang the man. But the final decision was to escort him out of the city limits and turn him loose.

S. J. Willis, who played the part of the deputy sheriff at the jail in St. Joseph, was given the chore of seeing the traitor out of town. The man disappeared. Willis was asked no questions. Years later, some people came to Lawrence, inquiring about their relative. He had never been heard from by his family.

Lawrence, Kansas paid a high price when Quantrill's raiders attacked the anti-slavery bastion in 1863. Page 14

II
1860 — 1869

The War Years

Quantrill's Raid on Olathe
Johnson County — 1862

William Clarke Quantrill was an enigma when the 1860 decade began. Born in Ohio in 1837, his sympathies seemed strongly anti-slavery when the question arose, as it did in almost every conversation. He even remarked once that he thought all Missourians should be shot. At that time he was teaching school in Kansas.

Then he took a job with Russell, Majors and Waddell on a wagon train to Salt Lake City. Most of the men driving the wagons were from Missouri. Quantrill began to change his opinions.

He had originally come to the frontier with some other settlers from Ohio. By 1860, he had dropped his Ohio friends and began to run with new friends from Missouri.

When war broke out, he went south where his sympathies had finally settled. He didn't like the confines of military life. He wanted to head up his own band. He organized a group of farmers along the Missouri border to fight back against Jayhawk raiders. That was his kind of fighting.

Quantrill's band struck the little town of Aubry, just inside Kansas. Then the Union

Kansas State Historical Society

William Quantrill

Army issued a proclamation declaring that the guerrillas were outlaws, not part of the Confederate Army, and should be shot on sight. That irritated people who had south-

Park Street, Olathe, Kansas

Kansas State Historical Society

ern sympathies and Quantrill benefited as more men joined him.

He struck hard at Union forces in Independence, Missouri, and took over the entire town. Quantrill was praised by the Confederate Army. He was given the rank of captain.

But Quantrill wanted none of the restrictions that went with being an army officer. He had his own band and worked better outside army regulations.

On September 6, 1862, his band crossed the border into Kansas and hit Olathe. This time it wasn't just a raid to destroy property. He went there to kill as well as loot. He took wagons to haul the loot away. But he found more than he could haul so he sent men to the farms around town to steal more teams and wagons. He didn't burn the town but he did leave six residents dead and everything in ruins.

Word of Quantrill's raid on Olathe spread quickly. When it reached Fort Leavenworth, the commander sent troops to run down Quantrill. They caught up with him in Cass County, Missouri, not far from the scene of the raid. Quantrill apparently had not expected the army to react so quickly.

Quantrill moved his men out and a running battle followed that lasted several days, according to reports. Two guerrillas were killed but there is no mention of army casualties. The army's goal was to capture and destroy Quantrill's raiders. But they all escaped except the two who were killed.

The soldiers did put an end to Quantrill's raiding for the moment. The guerrillas disbanded and scattered over Missouri.

The Undelivered Warnings Douglas County — 1863

It seems bizarre that so many things could happen to thwart good intentions and mighty efforts. It seemed that Lawrence, Kansas was doomed and nothing anybody could do could prevent it.

Quantrill and his raiders were closing in on Lawrence in the early morning hours of August 23, 1863, and some citizens guessed where he was going. He stopped at the Jennings farm for water. His men were thirsty. Mrs. Jennings wasn't sure how many men there were since it was very dark, just past midnight. But she was certain there were more than a hundred. It took a lot of water to quench their thirst.

Mr. Jennings was a captain in the Union Army and was stationed in Fort Smith,

Arkansas, so Mrs. Jennings had to cope with the situation on her own. When Quantrill's men satisfied their thirst, they went to another house not far from the Jennings farm. A man named Joseph Stone lived there with his wife and son.

At the Stone house, the men banged on the door until Mrs. Stone came out. They demanded that Mr. Stone guide them into Lawrence. The Stone family had moved to the area from Missouri to escape trouble there and the woman knew that if the raiders found her husband and son, they would kill them. So she used every excuse she could think of for not calling her husband.

One of the visitors named George Todd stepped forward and demanded that Joseph Stone come out. When he did come out, Todd recognized him as the man who had caused him to be arrested in Kansas City a couple of years earlier. When he identified Stone, the men behind the house came around front, knowing there was going to be some action. That left the back of the house unguarded and the son slipped out the window and hid in a corn field.

Todd wanted to kill Stone but Quantrill wouldn't allow any shooting so close to town. So Todd took Stone off a ways from the house. One report says that Todd took an old musket and beat Stone's brains out. Another says that, after he got Stone almost a mile from the house, he shot him.

The report says it was that shot that warned Mrs. Jennings that the visitors were killers and surely must be headed for Lawrence to kill and plunder. She started for her neighbor's place to get help. She didn't have a good horse but her neighbor, William Guest, did have one. She took her colored servant, Henry Thompson, and ran to Guest's house. (Some reports say Thompson was Guest's servant.)

Mrs. Jennings begged Guest to send Henry Thompson on a horse to Lawrence to warn the people of the approaching danger. There could be only one reason for so many men to be riding hard at that time of night. But Guest would not believe any such event was imminent and he refused to let his good horse be used on a wild goose chase.

Since she couldn't get Guest to loan his horse, Mrs. Jennings told Thompson to run to Eudora, Kansas, five miles closer to Lawrence, and get someone there to ride into town and warn the people. Thompson went, running as hard as he could.

Thompson had a moment of good luck when he came across the Justice of the Peace, Frederick Pilla, returning home from performing an evening wedding near Olathe. The Negro boy, eighteen years old, told Pilla why he was running for Eudora. Pilla took over and sent his buggy team flying into town.

In Eudora, Pilla woke the town and told everyone the news. Volunteers were called for to make the ride into Lawrence to warn the town. Three men stepped forward, led by the city marshal, David Kraus. The other two were Casper Marfelius and Jerry Reel.

They saddled their horses and headed for Lawrence. The marshal was thrown off his horse and injured before he got to the edge of town. He was taken to a house and his injuries doctored. The other two raced on, unaware that the marshal was not following them.

Reel had a fine Kentucky mare that could really run. But he didn't get far ahead of Marfelius. They raced through the night and it was nearing dawn when the long-legged black Kentucky mare missed a step and fell. Reel was crushed under the horse.

Marfelius stopped to pull Reel out from under his horse and take him to a nearby farm house where they tried to doctor him. Both Marfelius and Reel were out of the race because now it was too late to warn Lawrence. Reel died the next day from his injuries.

Four people had tried to warn Lawrence without success. But there was a fifth who came even closer.

A Shawnee Indian named Palathe came into Kansas City at midnight and heard a report that three hundred men were riding through the night. A scout named Bartles concluded that it was Quantrill and he was headed for Lawrence. There was some talk of trying to warn Lawrence, but no one thought there was any chance of beating Quantrill to the town. The Shawnee said he'd like to try.

Bartles had the best horses in the territory and he took the Shawnee to his place and let him pick a horse. It was a racer and the Shawnee was a good rider.

The Shawnee moved out, letting the horse run hard when the road was clear. The horse, a racer trained to give his best at all times, stretched out and ate up the miles. The Shawnee knew the country and he thought he had a chance of arriving in Lawrence before dawn. That would likely be the time Quantrill would strike, wanting to catch the townspeople asleep but still having enough light for the raiders to see what they were doing.

The rider was nearing his objective when the horse started to stagger. He stopped and let the animal catch its wind. When it could go on, he pushed his mount to its limit. It was getting light enough that he could see the row of trees that marked the edge of Lawrence.

The horse staggered again. It had run itself out. The Shawnee had to make a decision. He felt he still had a chance to warn the town before Quantrill got there. If he stopped, the horse might recover. If he drove it on, it would be ruined. He was racing to save lives so he didn't hesitate.

Frank James

Kansas State
Historical Society
Photos

Jesse James

Taking his knife, he cut open the hide on the horse's shoulders and rubbed in gun powder. The horse lunged forward in pain, racing harder than it had done all night.

But it was not to be. As it neared its destination, the horse stopped suddenly, reared, squalled mightily, and fell dead. The Shawnee hit the road running. He could see the streets now.

But even as he was trying to decide which street to take to deliver the warning to the people, Quantrill's men struck. The sounds of the yelling and shooting were loud in the Indian's ears. He was too late.

So many had tried to warn the town of its danger; some had come close. But in the end, they all failed.

Quantrill's Lawrence Raid Douglas County — 1863

There are enough stories about Quantrill's raid on Lawrence, Kansas to fill a book. A brief review of the event should be sufficient for most readers, with a quick look at a few individual stories that may be new to some.

Reports on the number of men with Quantrill range from 200 to 450. The number most often quoted is 350. The number of men killed in Lawrence most often reported is 143.

Quantrill's raiders rode into Lawrence at five o'clock in the morning on August 23, 1863. It was barely light enough for them to see where they were going. It was Quantrill's plan to hit the town before most of its citizens were awake and he caught them totally by surprise.

William Gregg, one of Quantrill's lieutenants, said later that they had come to Lawrence to kill and plunder. And they did exactly that. Killing 143 men practically wiped out the fighting force of the town.

One of the men Quantrill especially wanted to catch was General James H. Lane. But Lane wasn't in the south part of town where Quantrill entered that morning. Before Quantrill reached the area where Lane lived, the general escaped into a corn field and hid there until the raiders left town about nine o'clock.

Quantrill's force included several men who would later make their mark in the outlaw world. Perhaps the one who rode longest with Quantrill was Cole Younger. Cole's brother, Jim, was only fifteen when he joined Quantrill. He couldn't stand the ridicule that the Youngers were getting at home because Cole had turned outlaw so he ran off and joined his brother. He got in the gang just in time to go on the Lawrence raid.

Frank and Jesse James, brothers destined to become well known in the outlaw world also joined Quantrill. Frank often rode with Quantrill and Jesse did, too. But like Jim Younger, Jesse was only fifteen when he joined his brother shortly before the Lawrence raid. According to reports, it doesn't appear that Jesse was at Lawrence, but Frank James did go.

Quantrill had a list of people to kill and businesses to destroy in Lawrence. The newspaper, *The Tribune*, owned by John Speer, had published some strong articles against slavery in Kansas, proclaiming that Southern institution had no place in the state. Quantrill broke into the newspaper office and destroyed it, but he didn't find Speer.

Another newspaper that Quantrill hated was the *Kansas Free State*. He destroyed that paper and building then moved on to *The Republican*, a daily paper in which Speer had once owned a share. Quantrill silenced the main voices of the Free-Staters.

Captain George W. Bell was county clerk when Quantrill struck Lawrence. Bell had a wife and six children. When he heard the sound of the raiders destroying the town and killing its citizens, he grabbed his rifle and ran toward the noise, expecting to find the citizens fighting the raiders. But the surprise had been so great that no organized defense was possible. Seeing the situation, Bell climbed up on the roof of an unfinished building with another man. But they were seen.

Bell began to beg for the life of his companion when he discovered that the man he

Quantrill's raid
on Lawrence

was talking to was a man he had once called a friend. The two men climbed down. But a dozen other raiders demanded that the men from the roof be shot along with all the other men of town. Bell's friends objected but to no avail. Captain Bell and his companion were shot down, following Quantrill's orders.

Quantrill was very cautious on the way into town. As he led his men toward Lawrence, he warned them not to fire their guns. Any fight or disturbance would alert people to their movements and word might get to Lawrence. The success of his mission depended on surprise.

The raiders marched within half a mile of a company of Union troops at Aubry, on the Missouri-Kansas border. Quantrill's orders were not to fire unless fired upon. The Union soldiers did not fire so Quantrill's men marched silently past. A warning sent that early would surely have saved Lawrence.

As Quantrill's men left Lawrence, they were not so cautious. They marched past a

fine dairy farm. William and Mary Brown owned the farm and they didn't intend to let it be destroyed. But the raiders came out on the road that went past the Pleasant Hill Farm. William Brown saw them coming and thought he would join the neighborhood men in defending their places. He didn't know the extent of the damage to the town or the cruelty of the raiders. If he had, he wouldn't have left his wife and children on the farm.

But William did leave. Mary Brown saw that the raiders were setting all the houses on fire as they passed. Seeing how destructive they were, she ran into the corn field behind the barn with her children and hid.

The raiders reached the farm and a small group set fire to the corner of the house. Mary Brown left the children hidden in the cornfield and ran to the house and, scooping up dirt, threw it on the fire and put it out. The raiders stared at her but the leader of the little group waved them on.

Mrs. Brown saw more men coming down the same road and she ran back to calm her children. These men, seeing the house still standing, stopped and set another fire. Again, Mary Brown left the field and put out the fire. The raiders threatened to shoot her but she didn't hesitate. They didn't follow up on their threat.

They might have killed the woman if a diversion hadn't popped up. Two men came from a neighbor's barn which they had set on fire. They were dragging a Negro man. Their discussion was about how they were going to kill him. He claimed to be a free man.

Mary Brown had an old pistol that she had never fired. She wasn't even sure it worked. But she pointed it at the head of the man holding the Negro and shouted that she would kill him if he didn't let the Negro go.

Mary's audacity bewildered the men and they let the Negro go. They marched on to catch up with their comrades who had gone ahead. They knew falling too far behind could cost them their lives.

It was one of the very few victories that the people of Lawrence won over Quantrill's men that day. And a determined little woman deserved the credit.

The Tippie Gang
Crawford County — 1866

Immediately after the Civil War, outlaws gathered in gangs to prey on war widows and returning veterans before they could settle down again.

The Tippie Gang was really little more than three brothers and a few of their close friends. After they got organized, they worked out schemes to make big hauls. They found their fastest money came from buying cattle then stealing back the money from the sellers.

Posing as cattle buyers, Tippie Gang members went to farmers and ranchers who had cattle to sell. They bought the cattle, paid a good price and gave the owner his money, then drove the cattle away. After they had the cattle far enough away that they were safe from pursuit, some of the gang went back and robbed the owner of the money they had paid him. They got their money back and could safely sell the cattle, too, because they had a bill of sale.

The Tippie brothers lived in Linn County but they had worked all the way from Linn County through Bourbon County and into Crawford County.

Ralph Warner lived near Pittsburg and had a fine herd of cattle. He was planning to sell part of the herd and was talking to buyers. Among the buyers were three brothers. Warner had been tipped off that there was a gang of three brothers who bought cattle and then stole back the money.

So when the three Tippie brothers came to talk about buying Warner's cattle, he showed interest but stalled on making a deal. Before the Tippies returned, Warner passed the word that he was going to sell to the Tippies.

Only two of the brothers came to close the deal. They bought the cattle for a higher price than the other buyers would pay. The price didn't matter to them. They expected to get the money back, anyway.

About sundown, the two brothers and their helpers started the herd north toward Fort Scott. Warner didn't expect the gang to come back to steal his money before midnight or possibly not until the next day, allowing the drovers taking the herd north to get far enough away that no one could overtake them before they sold the cattle.

But his neighbors came over to help him watch, nevertheless.

In late evening, the watchers positioned around the outskirts of the yard, saw two men walking nonchalantly toward the house and guessed they were some friends or neighbors they didn't know. They didn't challenge them. They didn't recognize the danger until they heard gunfire.

Inside the house, the two gang members were surprised to find several men and even some women. They turned their guns on the men and demanded the money Warner had received for his cattle. It was in gold and in a sack.

Lem Shannon, Ralph Warner's brother-in-law, was cleaning his gun in preparation for the expected battle later in the night. Since he couldn't shoot his unloaded gun, he grabbed the nearest gunman. But before he could wrestle him to the floor, the man shot him, killing him instantly. Now the Tippie Gang was guilty of murder as well as theft.

Warner had no intention of letting his money get away. He grabbed the cash and dashed out into the night. Behind him, another neighbor, William Lamb, got his gun into action, slightly wounding one of the robbers.

The two robbers, surprised by the opposition in the house and seeing Warner escaping with the money, dashed outside in pursuit. But Warner was on familiar ground and, in the dark, he eluded the men. The robbers didn't hunt for him but made good their escape.

The men in the yard got their horses and tried to find the two killers. But they had to give up. Someone reminded them that the cattle hadn't been gone very long. Maybe they could catch up with the herd? They turned north as a heavy thunderstorm

Kansas State Historical Society
Joseph McCoy

rolled in and rain poured down. The riders kept going.

The Tippie brothers and their drovers had to stop the cattle and try to keep them from bolting in the storm.

Not far from Farlington, Kansas, some distance north of Pittsburg, the pursuers caught up with the herd as the drovers pushed toward Fort Scott. The thieves had no chance to get away.

The posse took the two Tippie brothers back to the little town of Monmouth. There they held a Judge Lynch court. Jacob Miller acted as judge.

While neither of the two Tippie brothers had fired the shot that killed Lem Shannon, in the eyes if the jury, they were judged guilty.

They hanged them on the spot.

That lynching had the desired effect. Not one of the Tippie gang showed up again in Crawford County or was ever identified with any other gang.

New Names in Kansas
Gove, Riley Counties — 1867

While Indian troubles dominated the scene in western Kansas, the eastern part of the state was beginning to rumble with new unrest. The days of Bleeding Kansas were past. The state had been established, the slavery question was settled, even though emotions still smoldered beneath the calm that the end of the war had forced on the populace. Many explosions of temper were laid to current events. But most people realized that the real root of the trouble was often the slow-to-die hatred that had fueled the Civil War.

New heroes and new villains filled the void left by the all-consuming fury of the war. Into that blank space came new names that would ride high in Kansas events for a long time.

The railroad was pushing west. There was competition between the railroad builders west from Kansas City and the one reaching out from Omaha, Nebraska. The first one to touch the one hundredth meridian would get the contract to go on across the continent, meeting the builders coming from the west coast. At first, the Kansas line was ahead and it looked as if it would be the winner. But a disgruntled worker shot and killed the man in charge of construction, leaving the project in disarray. The result was that the Nebraska line won the race.

But before the race was lost, the Kansas line put on more workers. That many men required a lot of food. A young man, good with a rifle, was hired to deliver meat for the big crew. He was an excellent shot and he

Kansas State Historical Society

James Butler (Wild Bill) Hickok

did the killing of the buffalo. Other workers butchered the animals and they kept the track laying crew well fed.

That man, William Cody, soon earned the reputation as the best hunter anywhere. He acquired the nickname that would follow him the rest of his life – Buffalo Bill.

Texas cattle were beginning to come north, seeking a market. After the war, Texas had thousands of cattle roaming the vast prairies. Many were unclaimed. And there was no market there for the cattle that did have owners.

Then word reached Texas that the railroad coming into Kansas would take the cat-

Lieutenant Colonel
George Armstrong Custer

tle to eastern markets where the price of beef was sky high. Two names began to circulate in Texas, one of a man and one of a town. Both spelled gold to men with cattle to sell. Joseph McCoy sent word down to Texas to bring up their cattle. And the place to bring them was Abilene.

Cattle running free on the Texas plains were branded and herded north. It was only a trickle of what would be coming in the years ahead. But no one had a hint of what else would come with the railroad and the cattle.

Railroad crews and railroad towns were considered rough. But they were Sunday school picnics compared to the towns that sprang up to welcome the Texas cattle and the men who brought them north.

The cowboys came off a trail drive of two months or more where they saw few people other than fellow drovers. They were ready to show the world what Texas men were made of. They got paid at the end of the drive and that money had to be spent. There were always plenty of greedy people at the end of the cattle drives ready to gobble up the money. Money, liquor and wild women made a combination that demanded more attention than ordinary town marshals could handle. That was when the other new names appeared in Kansas.

One of the many names that would make an indelible mark on the pages of Kansas history was just over the horizon. James Butler Hickok was about ready to step on stage as "Wild Bill" Hickok. One of the first stories about Hickok that caught the imagination of the public was one that might have had much to do with the nickname and of the man with the fast guns. Just how much of this story was fact and how much was the product of some overactive imagination seems difficult to ascertain.

No one had heard of the young man until an incident occurred near Manhattan, Kansas where Hickok was in charge of horses for a stage company. A band of thieves (listed in one story as ten in number) tried to steal them from Hickok. He put up a tremendous fight and, according to the story, when the fight ended, Hickok still had the horses and only one of the thieves was able to escape. The others were dead.

For a state struggling to forget the recent war and looking for new heroes, this man with the fast gun looked like a knight in shining armor. A new name had burned its brand on Kansas.

Ellis County Historical Society

William Comstock

Comstock Collects a Bad Debt
Wallace County — 1868

Another name that had a much shorter run in Kansas history than Hickok was William Comstock. Comstock was born in Michigan on January 27, 1842. Nothing is known of his father. His mother died when he was five and he went to live with two uncles in New York state. Next he moved in with his older sister in Wisconsin. He moved with that family to Omaha, Nebraska. From there, he went out on his own, still at a very young age. He showed up at Cottonwood Springs (near present day North Platte, Nebraska) as an Indian trader. He apparently spent quite a

Author's Photo

H. T. Wyatt's grave in the Ft. Wallace Cemetery

bit of time with the Indians. But familiarity does not always guarantee safety.

Comstock doesn't show up in history in any important role until he was twenty-four years old in 1866. By that time, he had become a valuable scout for the army and was assigned to the garrison at Fort Wallace in western Kansas.

Comstock rapidly developed a reputation as one of the best army scouts. Custer asked specifically for Comstock for his 1867 northern plains campaign. Later, in his book, *My Life on the Plains*, Custer wrote about Comstock:

"No Indian knew the country more thoroughly than did Comstock. He was perfectly familiar with every divide, water course and strip of timber for hundreds of miles in either direction. He knew the dress and peculiarities of every Indian tribe and spoke the language of many of them. Perfect in horsemanship, fearless in manner, a splendid hunter, and a gentleman by instinct, as modest and unassuming as he was brave, he was an interesting as well as valuable companion on a march such as was then before us."

When he wasn't scouting for the army, Comstock was at his Rose Creek ranch about eight miles west of Fort Wallace. In the winter, there were few campaigns and scouts were not in demand. Wood was a very scarce commodity in a country with so few trees. A man named Wyatt who contracted with Fort Wallace to supply wood for the winter was having trouble finding any. He came to Comstock for help. Comstock knew the country so well that Wyatt was sure he could tell him where to find wood he could cut. Comstock knew but he saw no need to give free information to the wood contractor. He thought that Wyatt should have located the wood before he promised to deliver it to the fort.

So Comstock made a deal with Wyatt. For a share of the profits, he would show Wyatt where to find wood. There was only one place in the area where wood could be found and that was over in Big Timbers, about twenty-five miles west of Fort Wallace.

Comstock took Wyatt to Big Timbers, a grove of giant cottonwood trees that looked out of place in this vast land of prairie grass. It was almost on the Colorado-Kansas line. The Big Timbers station on the Butterfield Overland Dispatch was there.

Wyatt fulfilled his contract with Fort Wallace, but refused to give Comstock a share.

The confrontation came in the sutler's store at Fort Wallace, owned by Val Todd. Wyatt was not a well liked man. He often bragged about belonging to Quantrill's raiders. There was a Cave Wyatt in Quantrill's raiders and this may have been the same man. Admitting he was one of

Kansas State Historical Society

Lieutenant Fred Beecher

Author's photo

A. L. (Sharp) Grover's grave at Ft. Wallace

Quantrill's men didn't set well with the Union soldiers at the post or with most of the area settlers. But that had nothing to do with Wyatt's refusal to live up to his bargain with Comstock.

The men exchanged hot words, and Wyatt turned and walked out of the store,

Fort Wallace — 1870

Kansas State Historical Society

emphasizing the finality of his refusal to pay Comstock.

Comstock shot Wyatt twice before he got off the porch and he stumbled and fell dead in the yard. Comstock was immediately arrested and taken to Hays City for trial.

The judge was the well known M. S. Joyce. Val Todd was there as a witness and he told what he saw. Comstock pleaded guilty. Judge Joyce asked Todd if the shooting was done with felonious intent. Todd said he had no idea what Comstock's intent was.

Turning to Comstock, the judge handed down his verdict.:

"Ye are a fool for tellin' it," the judge said. "I discharge ye for want of ividence."

Comstock Killed by Indians
Thomas County — 1868

The summer of 1868 brought more Indian unrest. The government had promised the tribes guns and ammunition so they could hunt. There was plenty of opposition to giving the Indians arms, but Indian Agent Wyncoop decided that it was safe because the Indians had promised faithfully that they would use them only for hunting buffalo for their winter meat.

On August 8, Wyncoop issued a hundred rifles, some pistols and 20,000 rounds of ammunition to the Indians. Two days later, the raids began on the Solomon River and the surrounding settlements. These were the raids that led to the September battle on the Arikaree River in northeastern Colorado.

Lieutenant Fred Beecher, who would lose his life at the Battle of Beecher Island on the Arikaree River, ordered his two scouts, Will Comstock and Abner Sharp Grover, to go to Turkey Leg's camp and ask for help to round up the culprits who had killed so many people on the Solomon.

The two scouts realized their danger but that didn't release them from their orders. They rode northwest to Turkey Leg's camp in what is now Thomas County. Both knew Turkey Leg and believed he could be trusted.

Before they got to Turkey Leg's camp on the upper reaches of the Solomon River, they heard some of the details of the raids on the Solomon and Saline Rivers. Most of the raiders had been Cheyenne. Turkey Leg and his warriors were Cheyenne. It intensified the danger of their visit.

They were greeted by Turkey Leg who assured them they were welcome in peace. But before the scouts left, a messenger came

Kansas State Historical Society

Trees were scarce on the plains. Railroad trestles often served as the gallows.

his horse. He pretended to be dead. The Indians had enough respect for their former friends not to scalp them.

When the Indians returned to their camp, Grover hid in some tall grass. He stayed there through the night and the next day started his painful way south. By flagging down a train east of Monument, he managed to get to that station and then on to Fort Wallace to report what had happened.

Sharp Grover recovered fast enough to go with Colonel Forsyth and his fifty scouts to chase the Indians and fight the battle of Beecher Island, a nine-day battle, in late September.

Grover survived that battle only to be killed later at Pond Creek. He was unarmed at the time.

Wild Times in Sheridan Logan County — 1868-1870

Few towns were wilder than Sheridan, Kansas, the end of the railroad track for almost two years. Sheridan grew out of the prairie from nothing. And it disappeared like a wisp of smoke when the railroad moved on.

In its short life, Sheridan reached a pinnacle of violence and corruption achieved in few places in such a limited time. The Kansas Pacific Railroad had reached that point when the money ran out. The railroad planned to build on west as soon as more money was available.

The stage line to western points began at Sheridan, as did the freight route. Bull trains and mule trains loaded there. Idle railroad workers swarmed over the town angry that they couldn't earn the wages that had sustained their earlier sprees. "Idle hands are the devil's tools," the old saying

into camp. They had no idea what his message was. If they had known, they would have realized their danger. Colonel Benteen and his men had caught some Indians in the act of raiding a farm on the Saline River and had given chase, killing three of the warriors.

Sensing the change in the Indians, the two scouts thanked their host and left. A short distance from the camp, several warriors caught up with them. The men thought the warriors were coming to assure their visitors safe passage from the area.

But just as the scouts began to relax, the Indians struck. Those behind the two scouts brought up their rifles and fired. Comstock was killed instantly. Grover was knocked off goes. Sheridan proved that adage with a vengeance.

The town had exploded on the prairie when the laying of track stopped. Fights and killings increased at an alarming rate. Before a single street was surveyed, the man who had been hired to do that work was called on to stake out a cemetery on the hill north of town. During the first week of its existence, the town put three residents in the new addition. "I'll give you a high lot," was a death threat in Sheridan.

Within weeks of the arrival of the first residents on July 25, 1868, the violence and mayhem in town forced the new business-men to take a stand. They organized a vigilance committee and gave notice to certain people by written letter to leave town within forty-eight hours.

Some people apparently felt they couldn't wait that long to be rid of some trouble-makers. The morning after the letters were sent out, three men were found hanging from the railroad trestle east of town. There were no trees around Sheridan. It was bare prairie. The only convenient hanging spot was the trestle.

Miguel Otero, whose father owned a large warehouse in Sheridan, was just a boy in those days. He wrote in later years that he used to run down the tracks every morning to see if he recognized any of the men hanging from the trestle.

Except for a few hotels and grocery and hardware stores, practically every business sold liquor, often in connection with a dance hall and brothel. There was no law in Sheridan except the law of the gun and it was frequently enforced.

The town was thirteen miles northeast of Fort Wallace (seventeen miles northeast of the town of Wallace). That was far enough from the soldiers to allow Indians to roam free. They attacked Sheridan's outskirts a few times. That added to the mayhem with-

in, and made life a precarious, if often an interesting, affair.

For the short time Sheridan existed, it earned the title of the "black-eye" of Kansas. A lot of people died in those two years. But no one expired because of boredom.

One reporter wrote for his newspaper that "Sheridan should be put under martial law. Human life is at a discount there. The scum of creation has congregated there and assumed control of municipal and social affairs. The vicious have taken possession of the town and reign supreme."

The population of Sheridan in its heyday was about two thousand people. Most of them were still there when the railroad built on west. But when Kit Carson, Colorado, became the end of track in May, 1870, the town of Sheridan packed up. First the railroad equipment moved, then the "devil's equipment," as one man called it, departed. A survey a month later showed only eighty people still in Sheridan and those were gone before the count was made official.

Neb, "The Devil's Own" Logan County — 1868

Towns like Sheridan produced some weird characters and equally weird stories. Neb is one such story.

Neb was a rather short man, looking a little overweight, probably because of his flushed heavy-featured face. One man said Neb reminded him of a complacent priest. But Sheridan knew him as a wild tiger, vicious if the situation called for it.

The town had seen his tantrums and was ready to blame any unsolved murder on Neb's rage.

One man decided one hot afternoon to enjoy a dip in the pool at the foot of the butte near town. The pool was actually in the bed of the North Fork of the Smoky Hill River.

The only known picture of Sheridan, Kansas.

Kansas State Historical Society

The town was built on the north bank of that stream.

The bather stripped down to his drawers and stepped into the water. On about the second step, his foot hit something slick and slimy. It didn't feel like a rock. Stooping, he discovered he had stepped on the face of a dead man. He was out of the water in less time than it takes to scream. With help, he fished the body out of the pool. It had been in the water for some time.

Rocks in the pockets of the clothes and a bag of rocks tied around the victim's neck had kept the body under water. In the palm of one hand was a card, the jack of spades, held there with a wooden splinter. Inquiry in town revealed that the murdered man had been a cheating gambler. Someone had killed him, then branded him with the Jack of Spades, and tossed him in the pool instead of burying him on the hill. Nobody knew who had done it, but Neb was the natural suspect. But most people thought the victim got what he deserved so nobody made any effort to find the killer. They felt that the death of such a character was a step toward respectability for Sheridan.

Neb seemed to get his trigger-happy temper rubbed backward almost every day and it erupted with the violence of a volcano. He usually carried a big revolver that never deteriorated from lack of use. He often was quite indiscriminate as he emptied the chambers of his gun. People ducked, then came out cautiously, swearing vengeance on Neb.

But Neb was never around. People were convinced that he could simply disappear into the prairie. He never came to town to eat. Some folks decided he must eat grass like Nebuchadnezzar, king of Babylon, who was driven outside the walls of the city to eat grass with the animals. Thus, the little wild-tempered man got his name of Neb. He always disappeared into the prairie whenever he had to run. Nobody would have been surprised to learn that he ate grass, too.

When he first came to Sheridan, Neb set himself up as a lawyer and notary. Within a week, he issued a divorce to a woman whose husband was away on a buffalo hunt. Then he married her to an emigrant heading west. When the husband came back, he went in search of Neb. That was the first time he disappeared like a shadow into the prairie. He was called on soon by the same buffalo hunter to marry him to a woman who had come searching for her eloping husband.

Neb escaped trouble that time. But soon a legitimate lawyer and a notary arrived in Sheridan. Neb was out of a job. That didn't seem to worry him. He tried his hand at several other occupations at which he was no better equipped than that of lawyer. But he was a good gambler and that was a very lucrative profession – if a man could win. And Neb did.

Neb was constantly getting into trouble then disappearing into the prairie before he had to pay the price. He made his run into the prairie so often that Sheridan added "the devil's own," to his name.

Neb began carrying a sixteen-shot Henry rifle whenever he came to town. The sight of the rifle stopped many an argument before it really began. One segment of the town was Irish, mostly workers who were waiting for the railroad construction to continue west. Neb got crosswise with the Irish community one day and from the edge of Irishtown, sprayed rifle bullets through that settlement. Everyone dived into cellars or behind buildings and fences – whatever was close that offered protection.

When Neb emptied the rifle, the Irish began coming out of their holes. They took after Neb – men, women and children. They intended to draw and quarter him if they caught him. But once again, Neb ran to the west out on the prairie and disappeared like a wisp of smoke. When the pursuers got to the top of the knoll where he was last seen, there was nothing but empty prairie before them.

Each Irishman had whatever weapon he could find. One woman even carried a small pig and was swinging it like a club. Another had a kettle half full of hot water. As they came back twenty minutes later, empty-

Author's photo

Ft. Wallace historical marker

handed, one was heard to say, "He's the devil's own, all right. One of his bullets clipped a lock of me hair."

The incident almost spelled the end of Neb. Men banded together and swore they would find and hang him. Then a government detective brought some men to the end of track, looking for a counterfeiter. He had traced some bad bills back to Sheridan. Everyone thought of Neb. Not that he ever had much money. But Neb was the root of everything evil in Sheridan, the way most people saw it. So why not counterfeiting, too?

They searched the town to no avail. Then someone remembered the ghost shack. The ghost had been reported a couple of times west of the hill, mostly by drunken Irishmen. So nobody paid much attention to the stories. But one man talked to three Irishmen who swore they had seen the ghost and he believed them. They came puffing into a saloon in town, white as sheets. The man based his conviction on the fact that those three Irishmen were dead sober when they got to town and he hadn't seen them sober in the previous two weeks.

There was as old abandoned shack over the hill where the ghost had been reported. Maybe the counterfeiter was there?

Several men accompanied the detective. The old dugout had a roof over the front part but it had partly caved in. There was no light in or around the dwelling. But that was to be expected. Counterfeiters didn't advertise their presence. The men formed a circle around the old shack and slowly closed in. Two members of the posse, wanting to stay out of any shooting that might erupt, got around behind the dugout.

When the posse members got closer to the dugout, they heard a moan. That was enough for most of them. But not for the detective. He stood his ground. So the other men came creeping back to prove they weren't cowards.

Cautiously, they advanced on the front of the dugout. Suddenly there was a bang near the two men who had chosen to stay on the "safe" side of the dugout. They wheeled to face a ghost wrapped in white.

One of the men swore afterward that he passed the other as they charged toward the trail back to town. But the other one insisted that nobody could have outrun him at that moment. The chief detective didn't run but jerked out his gun and shot at the ghost. That's when the mystery unraveled.

The ghost fell and somebody pulled off his sheet, revealing Neb. His sudden appearance was quickly explained.

The old dugout had been built by some Indian-wise homesteader before the railroad tracks reached the area. Like most builders alone on the plains, the pioneer dug a tunnel into the back of the dugout so he could escape if Indians attacked. At the end of the tunnel, he dug a hole up to the level of the prairie, placed a few rocks around it and a flat rock over them, leaving only a narrow

Kansas State Historical Society

Monument in Ft. Wallace Cemetery

slit through which guns could be fired. When Neb donned his ghost sheet and popped up next to the two men, they departed like scalded rats.

It was the other inhabitants of the dugout who really shocked the posse. Neb was down on the ground, wounded superficially. A young girl, about fifteen, was kneeling beside him, crying and calling him, "Papa." An old woman stood in the broken doorway begging the men not to harm an old lady.

The men learned that the girl was really Neb's daughter and he had hired the old lady to look after her. He didn't want his daughter on the streets of Sheridan. The men found no sign of counterfeiting. They dressed Neb's wounds, helped the trio get settled in their dugout, then went back to town.

The next day as the detective and some other men rode out of town on the train, they leaned out to see who had been hanged on the trestle where the track crossed the gully east of town. At least two dozen showed up under the trestle before Sheridan disappeared. The men were shocked to find Neb hanging there, swinging in the breeze, his face turned grotesquely upward as the train moved along.

One of the men sent word back to Sheridan to send the girl east and he would pay the expenses of her education. But she never came. The last they heard of her, she was seen walking the streets of Kit Carson, the next end of track town after Sheridan. As one man said, it would have been better if she had died along with her father.

Jes-so, the Dwarf
Logan County — 1869

There was a lot of living and dying crowded into Sheridan's two-year heyday.

One day Sharp Grover a plains veteran was in Sheridan. Homer Wheeler, a old-timer himself, was in town that day with Grover. A man who had just been discharged from the Fifth Cavalry was whooping it up. His reckless shooting was making life dangerous on the street.

Wheeler and Grover were in the barber-shop and Grover got up and went out on the sidewalk. He shouted at the ex-soldier to stop the shooting. The man yelled back for Grover to hunt his hole or he'd shoot him. He turned his gun toward Grover and the scout pulled his weapon and shot the man, killing him instantly. Then he turne... back inside the barbershop an... the chair, telling the barber to his work.

The shooting was another ordinary event in Sheridan. If it hadn't been for a newspaper reporter, it might have been forgotten entirely within a day or two.

The shooting preceded by only a short time the arrival of two people who, anywhere but in Sheridan, would have stirred a great deal of interest.

The man was middle-aged but that was the only normal thing about him. He was a dwarf with a normal sized head on his small hump-backed body. His left hand was withered and hung useless on his arm. But when a person looked into the dwarf's piercing eyes, he forgot all the other abnormalities. His eyes were like those of a stalking cat, darting around until they fixed on a target with a fierceness that defied description.

With the dwarf was a pretty Mexican girl, still in her mid-teens. He claimed she was his adopted daughter. When questioned, something the dwarf didn't like, it was learned that the girl had been a waif in New Mexico and he had picked her up and was determined to make a lady of her. They made an odd pair as they moved around town.

Most of the people would have been perfectly satisfied to leave the dwarf alone. He shunned all advances of friendship. But the girl was different. She bubbled with friendliness and laughter. The first week they were in Sheridan, the dwarf had a fight with a young man who insisted on getting acquainted with the girl.

Neither the dwarf nor his adopted daughter gave anybody a name. The dwarf inadvertently named himself. He had a habit of answering every question or state-

Small boys enjoy a flood during the early days of Abilene.

Kansas State Historical Society

ment with a mumbled, "Jes so," especially if he agreed with what was said. Some thought his name was Jesse and he was pronouncing it oddly. But they soon learned that "Jes-so" was his stock answer to anything said to him. So he became "Jes-so" to everyone.

It was considered dangerous to pry into Jes-so's private life. But there were those who dared try. Most were young men trying to get close to the girl. Her coquettish smiles made young men take risks. They learned that the dwarf had lost the use of his left hand when it was crushed under a heavy wagon wheel while he was rescuing the little girl.

There was no question about Jes-so's determination to protect his little girl from all danger, including the possessive eyes of the young men in town. Two fights in the first ten days proved that. Either the young men were reluctant to fight a hump-backed dwarf or he was a much better fighter than

they had expected. The dwarf won both fights and warned his opponents to stay away from his daughter.

Just two weeks after Jes-so arrived in Sheridan, he got up one morning and found his girl gone. He wandered around town most of the forenoon, inquiring about his daughter. Nobody had seen her. He was furious. As one man described him, "He crept around town like a wildcat whetting its claws on the gravelly soil, preparing to spring." The postmaster said there was "more hell" in his face than he ever expected to see on this earth.

The dwarf discovered that a young man named Bonny also was missing. He had fought with Bonny so he was sure that Bonny had taken the girl. The postmaster asked him if he was going after the couple. "Jes-so," the dwarf replied.

He disappeared at noon and, after a couple of days, he was almost forgotten. Very few happenings in Sheridan could hold the

Hays City 1868

attention of the public for long. Too many bizarre things were taking place.

Two weeks later, Sheridan residents were reminded of Jes-so and his mission, in the story told by a wagon master who brought in a train in from Santa Fe.

The wagon master had happened upon a strange scene at the crossing of the Purgatory River. There was an overturned feed box that formed a table. Two corpses sat at the table, one on either side, their heads bowed forward together. One was the corpse of a man; the other of a woman. There was a Catholic prayer book between them. The girl's hand was on the book and the man's hand was on top of her hand. It was a ghastly marriage performed by the murderer. Even residents of Sheridan could scarcely believe anyone could do such a thing.

But like all bizarre things that happened in and around Sheridan, it was soon forgotten. A month later, Jes-so returned to town. Only one person asked him if he had found the girl. His reply was the usual, "Jes-so."

Abilene, the First Cow Town
Dickinson County — 1868-1870

Texas men had gone to war from 1861 to 1865, leaving their farms and ranches unattended. Cattle ran wild, unbranded. There was no market in Texas for the cattle and no one even bothered to round them up.

Then Joseph McCoy arrived in Kansas with visions of creating a market for all those cattle in Texas. He went out west of Kansas City – far enough so there were no farmers to interfere with the passage of the cattle herds – and he started a town. He built loading pens near the tracks along the new railroad that was reaching out toward Denver. More importantly, the tracks also ran east to the markets McCoy hoped to reach with the cattle.

Then he sent messengers south to tell the Texans there was a market for their cattle if they would trail them to the railroad in Kansas. Abilene was the town.

A few herds came in 1867, enough to spread the word across Texas like a prairie fire. Round up those wild cattle and take them to Kansas and get rich! "Rich" was a word that fired up the cattlemen like gold sparked the prospector. Men began rounding up cattle. If the animals didn't have a brand, and most didn't, they were roped and branded by the man who caught them.

Then they headed north. The spring of 1868 brought big herds to Abilene. The town was almost swamped. There were five or six cowboys in town for every permanent citizen. And the cowboys ruled the roost.

The drovers had been on the trail for two or three months, enduring unexpected hardships. When the driven ended they had money to spend and no work to worry about. Few of the cowboys had any intention of taking their money home. And Abilene, suddenly infested with all the parasites looking for easy money, had no intention of letting the cowboys go home with any money. By fair means or foul, they intended to get it all.

The town was too young and too small to have any laws that could be enforced. One man reported that Abilene "had no jail, no court, no police control – everybody was free to drink, to gamble, to shoot to kill."

The *New York Tribune* sent out a reporter who wrote: "Gathered together in Abilene is the greatest collection of Texas cowboys, rascals, desperadoes and adventuresses the United States has ever known. There is no law, no restraint in this seething cauldron of vice and depravity."

Abilene was making its mark – but not exactly the mark that Joseph McCoy had in

Wild Bill Hickok

Kansas State Historical Society photos

Sam Strawhim

mind when he called for Texas cattle to come north.

Most of the cowboys were just looking for a good time. But after a cowboy had made a few too many trips to the bar, little arguments took on major proportions. Fists were suddenly beneath the dignity of a wealthy cowboy, which he considered himself to be. He wore his badge of courage in his holster and he didn't hesitate to use it.

Many a befuddled cowboy wound up in the nearby cemetery, the only peaceful place in or around the town.

By 1869, there were forty saloons in Abilene and, as one man said, "every saloon was equal to one dead cowboy." Whiskey was the prime culprit. Wild women were a reason for many gun battles. Gambling quarrels came in third in the race to kill off the cowboys.

Of course, only a small percent of the cowboys went in for the wild life. But, as has always been the case, a few bad apples spoil the whole barrel. To someone who hadn't been there before, it seemed that there was not one decent soul in Abilene.

In September 1869, the city fathers decided they had to bring order to the town. They incorporated and passed laws to be enforced when the spring cattle rush came. There were many new rules. But the one that made the cowboys roaring mad was the one that banned guns inside the city limits.

The cowboys resolved to show Abilene that it couldn't take their guns away. They quickly ran out the first marshals the town hired. They tore down the walls of the new jail before the roof was on. When the jail, under guard, was completed, they broke in and released the first cowboy incarcerated there.

Then the city hired Tom Smith to be marshal and the cowboy rebellion came to a painful halt early in the 1870s.

Hickok in Hays City
Ellis County — 1869

Hays City, Kansas sprang up beside the railroad when the tracks went past in 1867. From the very first, beginning with the railroad construction crews, Hays earned a reputation as a wild and dangerous place. The town tried to find a marshal or a county sheriff who could control the lawless element that seemed to gravitate to the town.

When the construction crews moved on, the buffalo hunters remained. They were reinforced by the soldiers from nearby Fort Hays. Saloons did a great business and gambling was out of control.

Then the town leaders thought they had found the solution to the problem. They hired James Butler Hickok to be the city marshal. Some reports said he was the sheriff. Wild Bill could clean up the town, they were sure.

It was Wild Bill's most important job up to that time, and he was determined to make good at it. There were some gunmen in town who let it be known that they didn't approve of a lawman poking his nose into their business.

Hickok's first clash was with a man named Mulvey (one paper said his name was Mulrey). The story went around town that Mulvey got the drop on Hickok and Hickok somehow distracted him long enough to pull his own gun and fire first. When the smoke cleared, Mulvey was ready for a peaceful spot in the new cemetery. Hickok had killed his first man as a law officer.

There was another troublemaker in town that the officials were more than eager to get rid of. Even the vigilance committee hadn't been able to dislodge him. His name was Sam Strawhim. Strawhim managed to avoid Hickok.

Then one day Hickok and his deputy, Pete Lanihan, were called to a saloon on Fort Street to put down a disturbance. They found the trouble was caused by Strawhim.

Strawhim resisted Hickok's effort to restrain him and a wild scuffle followed. Somehow in the scuffle, Hickok got his gun in his hand. No one seemed to know exactly how it happened but Strawhim got a bullet through the head. He was killed instantly.

An inquest was held. Perhaps the town's eagerness to get rid of Strawhim might have influenced the investigation a bit. Hickok was exonerated by a verdict of justified homicide.

Strawhim had friends in town and Hickok knew that his life was in danger if he got careless. He walked the streets cautiously and never stopped in a doorway where his silhouette would be clear to anyone outside the building.

When the election for sheriff was held the next fall, Hickok lost to his deputy, Pete Lanihan. Politics were very strong and Hickok was on the wrong side of the majority.

III
1870 — 1879

Wild Times

The Ladore Tragedy
Neosho County — May 10, 1870

In the little town of Ladore, Kansas, in southern Neosho County, tragedy struck suddenly and unexpectedly. It was a beautiful spring morning and the world seemed at peace. But Ladore's little world wasn't to stay that way.

Seven men rode into Ladore and dismounted. Then they scattered, each man going into a different store. Once inside, each man pulled a gun and ordered all the people in the store to hand over everything of value they had. Each robber had a sack to hold what he collected. Then the customers, along with the clerks and owners, were ordered out into the street.

They poured out of each establishment under the guns of the men who had entered the buildings a few minutes earlier. Three gunmen guarded the prisoners while the other four ransacked the homes and buildings they had missed in their initial charge. Within minutes, they had robbed every person in the business section of the little town.

But the raiders weren't finished. Mounting their horses, they thundered out of town, finally reining up and wheeling into the yard of the home of I. N. Roach. No one knows if it was by design or accident that they picked Roach's house.

Mr. Roach was home with his two daughters. The house was some distance from any neighbors. The outlaws charged inside and grabbed Roach. Dragging him outside, they beat him to death.

His daughters were horrified but they had little time to consider what they had seen. Leaving Roach's pulverized body, the outlaws grabbed the girls and dragged them outside where they mistreated them as only depraved men can do. When the intruders rode away, the girls were more dead than alive.

The outlaws left one of their own men, Bob Wright, dead in the yard, the victim of a fight among gang members.

In town, a posse was hastily organized and rushed after the outlaws. The men found the horrible situation in the Roach yard. With grim determination, they continued on the trail left by the six surviving outlaws.

The killers were either careless or confident that the beaten-down residents of the town would not follow them. The posse caught up with the outlaws and captured all six.

They took the captives back to town. There the residents, including the posse and the ones who had been unable to go on the search, lost no time in setting up a court. None of the once over-confident outlaws could doubt that this was a court that would be presided over by Judge Lynch.

The verdict came quickly with no dissenting votes. Five of the gang members, Dick Pitkin, William Ryan, Alex Matthews, Pat Riley, and one unnamed man, were dragged down to Labette Creek and hanged on a hackberry tree. The one surviving gang member, Pete Kelly, for some unexplained reason, was allowed to live. But six of the seven paid in full for their deeds.

The Man Who Tamed Abilene
Dickinson County — 1870

For two years, Abilene ran amuck. There were no laws in the town; at least, none that could be enforced. Being the first of the Kansas cattle towns, the residents had no idea how wild it could become. When the town council decided that laws had to be made, the rules were flaunted.

Abilene officials passed an ordinance banning all firearms within the town and started building a jail. No guns were checked in; the jail was torn down. The town hired guards and rebuilt the jail. The first man to be tossed into the new jail was a cook for a big cattle outfit. The cowboys found that having no cook was intolerable. They charged the jail, shot off the lock, and took their cook back to camp.

Abilene had become two towns. On the north side of the railroad tracks was the town that Joseph McCoy started. The law abiding citizens lived there and looked down their noses at those on the other side of the tracks. The south side of the tracks was

Tom Smith, the man who tamed Abilene

home to the element that catered to the Texas cowboys – saloons, hotels, dance halls. There was little else except for places that sold ammunition for the guns the cowboys were determined to carry.

In Texas Abilene, there was no law. In Kansas Abilene, there was as much law and order as the Texas cowboys would allow. The Texans usually stayed on their side of the tracks but, when they were well oiled up with liquor, they acknowledged no boundaries. They rode over the tracks and gave the gentler side of the town a sample of how the other half lived. That could not be tolerated by Kansas Abilene.

The town passed the new laws in the fall of 1869. But they were not to be enforced until the spring of 1870. Kansas Abilene felt that would give the Texans time to get used to the new rules, especially the one that required guns be checked as soon as the cowboys got inside the city limits.

The visitors from the south said little about the laws governing the saloons and the brothels. Both had to be licensed and pay taxes. That didn't bother the cowboys. But the way they saw it, the law that forbade them to wear their hardware in town cut right into their freedom. They had no intentions of obeying the order.

To enforce the law, the town officers sent to St. Louis for two men who had reputations for handling tough situations. Their coming was advertised and heralded as the beginning of the clean-up of Abilene. The Texans didn't ignore the warning. The day the tough law officers were scheduled to come in on the noon train, the cowboys planned a greeting for them.

They put on their best show of drinking, gambling, and shooting up the town. The officers moved around, taking in all the show. But when the midnight train pulled out for the east, the two "tough" law officers were on it, heading back to St. Louis.

A day earlier, a man named Tom Smith had ridden into Abilene and applied for the marshal job. He was told that the town had already hired two men who would handle everything with great efficiency. Smith left town, heading west to look for another job.

Abilene Mayor T. C. Henry, totally embarrassed by the sudden departure of his two hand-picked men, sent telegrams to every station to the west, trying to find Tom Smith. Smith had told Henry that he could handle the situation. Henry was now willing to give him a try.

One of the telegrams was delivered to Smith at Ellis, just west of Fort Harker. He held no animosity for the way he had been turned away when he applied for the job. He simply rode out of Ellis the next morning, heading back to Abilene.

Smith arrived in Abilene on June 4 and went immediately to see Mayor Henry. He was offered $150 a month to handle the job. Henry didn't want to get crossed up like he had with the St. Louis men. So he told Smith to look over Texas Street then come back and they'd talk if he still wanted the job.

Tom Smith was back in the mayor's office later in the afternoon. The mayor offered to back off on the order to force the cowboys to check their guns when they came into town. Smith disagreed. He said that there was no way anybody could control the town if the cowboys were allowed to remain armed. So the mayor reluctantly agreed to make new posters and have them posted everywhere stating all visitors must check their guns at a saloon or the mayor's office when they arrived in town.

The posters were made and tacked all over town. Even the hotels and brothels had the signs on their doors.

Businessmen in Texas Abilene could scarcely believe their eyes the next morning when they saw the signs. But their astonishment was mild compared to the reaction of the cowboys.

Before that first day was over, Tom Smith got his first challenge on the new law. It came in the form of a huge Texas cowboy called Big Hank. Smith had heard around town that Big Hank was bragging that no lawman could take his gun away from him — the man would be dead before he ever touched Hank's gun. Smith had been warned that Big Hank was an obnoxious braggart but very dangerous, nevertheless.

As he patrolled the streets, Smith saw a big man coming his way and guessed it was Big Hank. Tom Smith usually did all his patrolling from the back of a horse. But he dismounted to meet Big Hank on a level stage.

Hank welcomed the encounter and when he was close to Smith, demanded to know what he was going to do about his so-called gun law. Smith calmly replied that he was going to enforce it. Then he asked for Big Hank's gun.

Hank swore and dared Smith to take it. Smith calmly repeated his demand that Big Hank turn over his gun. That request met with profanity and verbal abuse.

Like the strike of a snake, Tom Smith leaped forward, crashing a fist into Hank's face. Hank staggered back as Smith snatched Hank's gun from its holster.

Smith then ordered Big Hank to get out of town and never show his face in Abilene again. Suddenly scared and totally embarrassed, Hank turned and staggered away.

No one in Abilene had ever seen anything like that. But nobody had ever seen anyone like Tom Smith.

Tom Smith was born in the lower east side of New York City. He sold newspapers on the street. On more than one occasion, when bigger boys tried to rob him of his money, he beat the daylights out of them. A fight promoter saw one of those fights, put Tom under contract and made him into a professional fighter.

Tom was soon earning as much as $750 a fight and was billed as the "Newsboy Terror." But his mother didn't like fighting and, on her deathbed, got a promise from her son to give up fighting. But he never lost his ability to handle with his fists men who were twice his size. He took that talent with him when he went west.

His first job in the West was as a wagon driver and guard for an army regiment in Arizona. Then he hauled freight for railroad construction crews. That led him to Bear River, Wyoming, where his anger was stirred by the gamblers and outright swindlers who were cheating the workers out of their paychecks. He organized the men who had been cheated and led them in a club swinging raid on the crooks, destroy-

Ellis County Historical Society
Fort Fletcher was later renamed Fort Hays

ing their headquarters and driving them out of town. He suddenly had a reputation for handling the bad men and the nickname of Bear River Tom. However, there were few in Abilene who had ever heard of Bear River Tom. They were soon to get acquainted.

News of Big Hank's humiliation spread over town like a blast of winter wind. Cowboys who had relied on Big Hank to either kill or humiliate Smith, looked for a reason. They finally decided that Smith had somehow gotten the jump on Hank. He couldn't do that again. They'd be watching for any quick moves the next time anyone faced him.

Another big cowboy called Wyoming Frank, who considered himself the equal of Big Hank, accepted the challenge and made a big wager that he could face down the marshal and come away with his gun. He walked the streets, bragging that he would take care of the marshal.

Tom Smith heard that Wyoming Frank was looking for him. But Smith didn't make an appearance until almost noon. Before that time, Frank was making the rounds of the saloons, claiming Smith had heard he was in town looking for him and had lit out. Abilene was free of the marshal and the cowboys had control again.

Just before noon, Smith came down the street, on foot again. Wyoming Frank went to meet him. Frank tried insults to get Smith to go for his gun. But the marshal only walked slowly toward him, demanding that he turn over his gun.

Frank stared into the marshal's cold gray eyes and backed off a few steps. Smith continued walking slowly forward, repeating his demand. Frank back-peddled until he had retreated into one of the saloons. Smith kept right after him.

Finally Frank backed into the bar where he could retreat no farther. A big crowd had followed the two into the saloon. A lot depended on the outcome of this confrontation.

No longer able to retreat, Frank exploded with a string of oaths. Suddenly, without warning, Smith leaped forward, smashing a fist into the big Texan's face. The blow slammed Frank against the bar and he slid to the floor. Smith stood astraddle of him, jerked the gun out of his holster, then gave him the same warning he had given Big Hank. He was never to show his face in Abilene again.

That was enough for the cowboys witnessing the scene. Guns were handed forward and the bartender tagged them with the names of the owners and put them on a back shelf where they could be retrieved when the cowboys left town.

Abilene settled down to as nearly a law abiding town as one could be with the herds of cattle coming up the trail to be shipped east. One other incident gives another glimpse of the effectiveness of Tom Smith as town marshal.

A Mexican cowboy started racing up and down Texas Street, endangering anyone within his reach. Smith heard the uproar and he stepped out of a doorway as the Mexican raced by. He grabbed the rider's leg in one hand and the horn of the saddle in the

other and threw the pony off balance. The horse and rider crashed on their sides in the street. The racing was over.

No matter who came before Tom Smith or followed him, there can be no doubt about who tamed Abilene.

Vigilante Justice
Butler, Cowley Counties — 1870

On the southern edge of Butler County, southeast of Wichita, a band of horse thieves began operations near the town of Douglass, Kansas. Their range reached to the south into Cowley County, almost to the town of Winfield.

At first, the gang's operations were small. Then they made off with a herd of two hundred and fifty mules. That was too much; they had to be stopped and a vigilance committee was organized.

Not knowing where the thieves had taken the mules, the vigilantes waited until they knew some of the culprits had returned to the area. They located four of the rustlers in a house near Douglass. The scouts for the vigilantes were positive these were four of the men they wanted. The vigilantes surrounded the house and demanded that the men come out. There was some reluctance before one man finally stepped out.

The other three refused to come out and a battle erupted. The vigilantes fired into the house from all sides. When the shooting stopped, they examined their work and discovered that they had killed all three who had refused to give up.

They questioned the one captive and apparently got the names of most of the gang who had done the stealing. It was a big gang. But the captive's revelation of the names of other members of the gang did not earn him an escape from the rope. Down along Walnut Creek, they hanged him. The vigilantes left the body on the river bank with a big sign, notifying any who saw it that he had been killed for stealing horses and mules.

The list of gang members showed several living right in Douglass. After some time, the vigilantes met again and they rounded up four of those in Douglass and took them down by an old mill and hanged them.

The Douglass paper published the names of all the undesirables who were still running free who were members of the horse stealing gang.

Several men suddenly left the country and Butler and Cowley counties were free of that gang of horse thieves.

The Killing of Tom Smith
Dickenson County —
November 2, 1870

Tom Smith held Abilene in check through the summer and fall of 1870. No one doubted that his law was supreme.

Then an event that apparently had no bearing on Smith took place in late October about ten miles northeast of Abilene. A Scotsman named Andrew McConnell came back to his dugout after being out hunting. He found his neighbor, John Shea, trying to drive his cattle out of McConnell's field where they had gone after breaking out of Shea's pasture.

McConnell had a hot temper and he was furious at finding Shea's cattle in his field. He screamed at Shea and Shea responded in like manner. McConnell used the gun he'd been hunting with and shot Shea, killing him.

Moses Miles, a neighbor and friend of McConnell's, saw what had happened and, along with McConnell, reported the killing to the authorities, claiming that it was self defense.

The matter was dropped until other neighbors of McConnell reported to the sheriff that it had not been self defense and offered proof.

A warrant for the arrest of McConnell and Miles was given to Sheriff Joseph Cramer. But when he and his deputy went to McConnell's place, they were driven off.

The sheriff apparently had all he wanted of McConnell. It was his deputy, J. H. McDonald, who recruited the town marshal, Tom Smith, to go with him to arrest McConnell and Miles.

They found the two neighbors armed and waiting for them. Smith said he had a warrant for McConnell's arrest. McConnell simply turned his rifle on Smith and shot him through the lung. Smith shot back and wounded the Scotsman.

The deputy sheriff, McDonald, turned and ran. That left Miles free to help his friend, McConnell. Smith and McConnell were grappling, both wounded but neither giving up.

Miles hit Smith over the head with his gun and then grabbed an ax and hit him with that, killing Smith.

The deputy sheriff, McDonald, rode back to town and reported what had happened. A posse was quickly organized and went after the two killers. They followed the trail past Junction City and, finally, northwest of Clay Center, they captured them.

Feelings were so high in Abilene against the two men that they had to move the trial to Manhattan in Riley County. Both men were found guilty. Miles, the one who wielded the ax that killed Smith, was sentenced to sixteen years in prison. McConnell was sentenced to twelve years.

Kansas State Historical Society

John Wesley Hardin

The funeral for Tom Smith, the man who tamed Abilene, was one of the grandest ever held in the town.

Bluff City Killing
Harper County — July, 1871

The trouble began at a trail camp just outside Newton, Kansas. Two cowboys got into an argument. One was Bill Cohron; the other a Mexican cowboy named Bideno. The quarrel ended when Bideno shot and killed Cohron.

The episode would probably have ended there and been forgotten except that Bill Cohron was a good friend of John Wesley Hardin.

Bideno headed south on his fastest horse when he learned that Hardin had a warrant for his arrest and was after him. At every opportunity, Bideno changed horses, trying to throw Hardin off his trail. At last, the Mexican was certain he had escaped from Hardin's pursuit and he stopped in the tiny town of Bluff City, almost on the Oklahoma border. He went into a restaurant to get a meal, the first he'd had since he started running. While he was eating, Hardin came in.

There are two versions of what happened next. Hardin said later that he gave Bideno a chance to surrender then shot him when he refused. The other version claimed that Hardin stepped into the restaurant and, without giving Bideno a chance to go for his gun, shot him. The one thing about which there was no argument was that Bideno had a bullet hole right in the center of his forehead.

Hardin was unknown in little Bluff City and he would have been in trouble if he had not had the warrant for Bideno's arrest. Hardin gave the mayor some money to pay for burying the dead cowboy and then he left, letting the little town settle back into its quiet existence.

The Newton Killings
Harvey County — August, 1871

Newton, Kansas sprang up while still waiting for the railroad tracks to come. Joseph McCoy, who put Abilene on the map, came to the new town and set up the stockyards and loading pens. Guided by the experience he had gained in Abilene, McCoy built what he considered to be the best yards and pens in Kansas. He had no doubt that Newton would become a bustling city.

Farmers around Abilene had doomed that town as a cattle shipping point. They put fences around their farms that blocked the trails of the cattle to the stockyards. There just wasn't room for both the farmers and all the cattle that were coming up from Texas. The Texas drives had to find a new market farther west where the farmers had not arrived to plow up the grass.

When the tracks came to Newton, the yards and pens were ready. The town was getting prepared, too. Hotels, saloons and dance halls sprang up like mushrooms. Gamblers, whiskey venders, soiled doves, descended on Newton.

Trouble began in August. There was an election on a railroad bond. Among the special police for the day was a man named William Bailey. He was very obnoxious and abusive and many people were disgusted with him. Most people knew he was a "Texas desperado" who had murdered three men. But he was needed on the special police force and he gladly took the job.

One of the men he insulted and pushed around that day was Mike McCluskie, a railroad man, and not one to take insults. In a drunken brawl the next day, Saturday, August 12, Bailey and McCluskie squared off. McCluskie killed Bailey.

McCluskie hurried out of town. But there was no need for flight. Most people felt that what he did was justified. No attempt was made to find him.

But that episode was the spark that started the pot to boiling. There was a saying among people of the new town that they had a killing a week. Now that Bailey had been killed, there would be another killing on or before next Saturday.

With uncanny accuracy, the prediction came true. One week later on Saturday night (actually 2 A.M. Sunday morning), the pot boiled over.

A man who was an eye witness to the happenings that night described what happened and also illustrated the tedious (though colorful at times) way news was reported in the 1870s. The writer was a correspondent for the *New York World* who happened to be in Newton that fateful night. He directed his story to the editor of the *Topeka Commonwealth*.

"Newton, August 21, 1871

"To the editor of the Commonwealth:

"The air of Newton is tainted with the hot steam of human blood. Murder, 'most foul and unnatural,' has again stained the pages of her short history and the brand of Cain is stamped in crimson characters on the foreheads of men with horrible frequency.

"The cessation of travel on the railroad and the want of telegraphic communication from this town on the Sabbath, have prevented the data contained in this letter from reaching you until the present date but your readers will have as prompt and complete a narrative as is possible under the circumstances.

"Your exhaustive and highly graphic article of a few days since, in which Newton, and particularly that part of it known as 'Hide Park,' appeared as the central figure, created a flutter of excitement in this community and, not withstanding the caustic, even stern, criticism on the general looseness of morals and disregard of both state and municipal laws, the almost unanimous verdict was that it was 'true, temperate and unbiased.'

Old depot at
Newton, Kansas.

"It will be remembered that about ten days since a Texas desperado by the name of Bailey, a man who is reputed to have killed at least two men in drunken brawls, met his death while murderously assaulting one McCluskie, lately in the employ of the Atchison, Topeka & Santa Fe Railroad. The common belief is, and the probabilities are, that McCluskie fired the fatal shot; whether true or not, however, such was the impression thus obtained among the Texas men, nearly all of whom in this vicinity, are cattle owners or drivers. These latter are a large and distinctive element of the population and though generally of a rough and forbidding exterior, still show some sterling qualities of character; standing by one another with a dogged obstinacy that might be called chivalrous, were it not so often exercised in a bad cause. The deceased was popular among his fellows. Good natured, generous, dangerous only when maddened by liquor, his bad qualities were forgotten and Texas sympathy was oblivious to ought but what endeared him to them. Sympathy, strengthened by bad counsels, intensified itself into rage; rage feeding on itself, verged into revenge; revenge, muttered and whispered and finally outspoken, culminated in murder.

"Of murder, we have now to deal. It was past midnight. The moon had sought her couch, and the stars alone were nature's watchers. Away out on the prairie from among a cluster of low roofed houses, twinkled lights and issued sounds of revelry and mirth. The town was buried in repose and naught animate was visible save an occasional pedestrian, hurrying home or the ghostly outline of a distant horseman returning to his camp.

"To the casual looker-on, the scene was bewitching: bewitching through its quietness and natural beauty: bewitching through its promise of quiet and rest. Of a sudden, however, the scene changes. Groups of men walking hastily and conversing in low, hurried tones, are seen approaching the town along the road leading to the place where the lights still twinkle and the sound of mirth flows on unbroken.

"Of what are they talking?

" 'There will be a fracas tonight, boys, and Mac is a dead man,' says one, a heavily bearded man, around whom his companions cluster in respectful attention. 'Texas is on the rampage tonight in dead earnest, and before morning there will be lively music over yonder,' pointing with his thumb to the place they had just left. 'We haven't more than quit in time. I would have told Mac, but they were watching me, and I didn't get a chance.'

"Another group crosses the railroad track and pauses to look back. 'I shouldn't wonder but what there will be shooting at Perry's before long,' remarks one. 'I know it,' says another. 'And I,'; 'And I,'; so echo the rest. 'The boys have sworn to kill McCluskie and they are going to do it tonight. You see if they don't,' says a bushy-haired man, with two revolvers in his belt, and a huge bowie knife protruding from his shirt front. These were Texans who knew what was on foot, but who by their criminal silence, have made themselves 'accessories before the fact'.

"Still groups and stragglers come along the road, the majority talking in the same vein, and nearly all actuated by the one motive of self preservation. They wanted to take no risk of chance bullets, and they hurried away. But did anyone try to avert the impending danger? No, not one. 'It's no business of mine,' was the common sentiment. 'Every one for himself, and the devil for the hindmost.' 'I'm sorry but it can't be helped.'

"A walk of a few moments brings us to the dance houses, one kept by Perry Tuttle, and another, the Alamo, by F. P. Cram (Kram). They are but thirty yards apart and around them are the other houses, built and used for purposes for which the reader can divine without unnecessary explanation. Women are the attraction. The grass is stubbed and yellow hereabouts and dim lanes radiate in every direction. Men are continually coming from one house to the other to seek occasionally a change of music but oftener a fresh partner. The proprietors of these houses are all men who have many friends and who by their personal qualities, are universally popular. Quiet, never intoxicated, and generous to a fault, their constant aim has been to keep quiet and orderly establishments; and they or their employees have always suppressed any signs of tumult or disorder immediately on their inception. It must be said to their credit that no disturbance would ever occur could their efforts quell it. One of the houses, the Alamo, had closed shortly after midnight. The musicians had been discharged and business for the night was over. In the other house, the dance was prolonged until after one o'clock when, the crowd thinning out, the proprietor gave the signal for closing.

"Now begins the tragedy. The victim was ready and the sacrificial priests stood waiting to receive him. The victim was Mike McCluskie, or, as he afterwards on his deathbed stated his name to be Arthur Delaney. The priests were all Texans, Hugh Anderson, Salado, Belle County, Texas; Jim Martin, Refugio, Texas; William Garrett, Salado, Texas; Henry Kearnes, Texas; Jim Wilkerson, Kentucky; and J. C. U., Salado, Texas. One of the priests sat talking to the victim with the evident intention of distracting his attention in order to allow one of the order to give the death blow. The others stood back watching and waiting for the entrance of the high priest, their eyes roving alternately from the victim to the door. The high priest enters and, striding along the room, confronts the victim and begins the death song. His weapon in his hand, with death looking grimly from its muzzle. His words come hot and hissing, beginning low and rising with his passion until they are shrieked out with demoniacal force. 'You are a cowardly s—n of a b—h! I will blow the top of your head off!' are the words that fall from his lips, at the same time the hammer falls and a ball goes crashing through the neck of the victim. The latter rises partially to his feet and presenting his weapon full at the breast of his adversary, presses the trigger. Malediction! The cap hangs fire and the victim, bathed in his own blood, but still discharging his weapon, falls to the floor. The high priest now gives the death stroke and reaching over, again taps the fountain of life by sending another bullet through the back of the prostrate man. The work is done, that is, partially.

"As the leader rises to his feet, the attendant priests discharge their weapons. Whether they found another victim, no one can say. Murder has

already accomplished its mission, and the days of McCluskie are numbered.

"But there is an avenging Nemesis on the track. A stalwart figure suddenly appears on the scene. For an instant, he remains motionless as if studying the situation. Then a sheet of flame vomits forth, apparently from his hand and a Texan staggers from the room, across the area, and falls dead at the door of the Alamo. Another and another and another shot follows until six men, all priests, have bowed to his prowess.

"There were others injured, one, Patrick Lee, a brakeman on the railroad, who was a quiet and inoffensive looker-on, shot through the bowels, and another, a shoveler on the same road, wounded in the leg.

"There was work enough for the doctors. The only two in town were immediately summoned. They were Drs. Caston and Boyd, and they were untiring in their professional efforts.

"By the time they arrived, the dead man, Martin, had been taken into the Alamo, where he lay saturated in his own blood. McCluskie had been carried upstairs as soon as he was shot. both dance houses were turned into hospitals. The dying and wounded have received every care and attention. The women nursed them with touching assiduity and tenderness. The floors and sides of both halls were everywhere sprinkled with blood, and gory stains yet remain. The magistrate of Newton declares his intention to suppress all dance houses in the future. Many question his authority to do so but the citizens will nearly all support him in case a demonstration is made to that effect. Coroner S. C. Bowman held an inquest over the remains of Martin

Hardin's fight with the Mexican drovers.

Kansas State Historical Society

THE FIGHT WITH THE MEXICAN HERDERS.

and McCluskie yesterday morning and a verdict was returned that Martin came to his death at the hands of some person unknown and that McCluskie came to his death at 8 o'clock AM this 20th day of August, by a shot from a pistol in the hands of Hugh Anderson, and that the said shooting was done feloniously and with intent to kill McCluskie. A warrant was accordingly issued by Marshal Harry Nevill for the arrest of Hugh Anderson.

"The following is a list of the men who suffered in the fracas: Arthur Delaney, St. Louis, neck, back and leg, dead; Jim Martin, neck, dead; Hugh Anderson, high priest, thigh and leg, doing fairly; Patrick Lee, bowels, critical; Jim Wilkerson, nose, slight, leg, slight; Henry Kearnes, right breast, fatal; William Garrett, shoulder and breast, fatal."

Most of the information about the killings is in the above report but it took the reporter, who signed his name "Allesan," two thousand words to tell a two hundred word story.

The reporter apparently didn't know who the "avenging Nemesis" was. He was Jim Riley, a good friend of Mike McCluskie. The battle was a series of revenge wars.

Hugh Anderson was getting revenge on McCluskie for killing a fellow Texan, William Bailey. Riley was taking revenge on Anderson and his men for killing Riley's friend, Mike McCluskie (Arthur Delaney).

Jim Riley disappeared and nothing more was heard of him.

Hugh Anderson was more seriously injured than the New York reporter stated. Facing the warrant for his arrest for the cold-blooded murder of Mike McCluskie, his fate seemed sealed. But Anderson's father came for him and, with plenty of help from other Texans and a few townspeople who had seen all the killing they wanted, he connived to slip him out of the room where he was bedfast by carrying him on a litter to the railroad depot after dark. They put him in a car already prepared for the scheme. He was locked in the closet so the marshal, who inspected every train before its departure, wouldn't find him. He rode out of Newton where certain death faced him but the general consensus was that he wouldn't survive his wounds, anyway. But he did – for a season.

Hardin vs. the Drovers
Sedgwick County — 1871

Sometimes there are stories that don't seem quite logical. But when John Wesley Hardin was involved, there is always the possibility that it is true.

One of those stories was centered just south of Newton, probably in the northern edge of Sedgwick County. One report says that Hardin, although only eighteen, was in charge of the cattle drive. Another says he was one of the drovers but definitely the fastest man in the crew with a gun. The latter sounds more logical.

Another trail herd was just behind Hardin's outfit and it was being driven by a Mexican crew. They kept crowding Hardin's herd so close that the cattle often mixed and they had to sort them out. Hardin's outfit quickly grew tired of the pressure. They were sure the Mexicans were crowding in, hoping to get some of Hardin's cattle mixed with theirs and they could get away with them.

Hardin rode back twice and warned the drovers to keep their herd back a safe distance from his. But they laughed at him. The last time he faced them, the foreman threatened to shoot Hardin if he came back again.

Even at that age, Hardin was not about to back off from such a challenge. He took his buddy, Jim Clements, with him when he went back. Clements was a good hand with a gun, too. Some of the crew offered to come along but Hardin shook his head. He was confident the two of them could face down the six cowboys who were crowding them.

When the Mexican drovers saw Hardin and Clements coming, they spurred their horses out in front of their cattle to meet the visitors.

There were no preliminaries this time. The gauntlet already had been throw. Now it was time to get things straightened out.

Hardin and Clements suddenly spurred their horses forward at top speed, their guns in their hands. The Mexicans charged to meet them, confidence in their superior numbers driving them.

Guns roared and dust churned up in a choking cloud as the two groups clashed. It was impossible to see just what was going on. But Hardin and Clements kept their bearings and kept shooting.

When the dust settled, all six of the opponents were off their horses and on the ground. According to the report, neither Hardin nor Clements had a scratch. That last statement is a bit hard to believe. But the fact does remain that Hardin and Clements won the battle and the Mexicans were dead losers.

Hickok Shoots Coe & Williams
Dickinson County —
October 5, 1871

James Butler Hickok figured prominently in the making of Kansas history in the 1870s. While an officer in Hays, he killed two men, Bill Mulvey and Sam Strawhim. He was establishing himself as one of the top law officers and fast gun handlers in the lawless towns of Kansas. But then he lost the election for sheriff in Hays and he was out of a job.

It was then that Abilene called for his services. He was sworn in as marshal of Abilene by the town's founder and mayor, Joseph McCoy. Abilene was coming into its last days as a cow town although no one knew it or, if they did, they wouldn't admit it. Too many homesteaders were plowing up the grass and fencing off the trails that the cattle used to get to the shipping pens in Abilene. But for the summer of 1871, it was still the wild town that the Texas drovers

First house in Independence, Kansas.

longed for from the time they left the Texas plains.

For some time, Hickok had it easy in Abilene. When things finally exploded, it came as a surprise to everyone.

It was October 5 and the season was virtually over. Even the people of Abilene could see the signs now. The cattle drives were not going to be coming up much longer. The citizens of the town and the farmers surrounding the town had had about all they could handle of the celebrations of the Texas cowboys when they reached the end of the trail.

Some of the rules of the town were being relaxed. Carrying a gun was no longer grounds for arrest. But firing a gun within the city limits was still prohibited.

Gambler Phil Coe broke that law. Maybe he was just letting off steam at the end of the season. There wouldn't be any Texas money flowing across the table to him for some time. At any rate, he fired his gun, apparently at nothing in particular, and that brought Wild Bill down to put a stop to that nonsense.

Hickok found Coe and demanded to know why he had fired his gun. Coe said he was shooting at a stray dog. But then he turned his gun on Hickok. There seemed to be no logical reason for this action unless he had a grudge against Hickok that no one knew about.

Hickok was never slow to respond to a challenge. His shots were ahead of Coe's. They stopped the gambler in his tracks. But then Mike Williams, Hickok's deputy, came running around the corner to help out. Maybe Hickok didn't recognize his deputy and thought he was some friend of Coe's coming to help the gambler. Or possibly Hickok's last two bullets were meant for Coe. They hit and killed Mike Williams. Neither Coe nor Williams were killed instantly, but both died before morning.

Hickok was devastated over the accidental shooting of his friend and deputy. He suddenly wanted to get away from the job that required such instant decisions and action.

He left Abilene and, for a short time, turned his attention to another friend, Buffalo Bill Cody, and joined his show.

The Bloody Benders
Labette County — 1871-1873

There are many stories of Kansas killers. But few can rival the brutal, emotionless murders that took place in southeastern Kansas over a span of less than two years from 1871 to 1873. As one writer said in introducing the story of the Benders: "In the flow of the generations of men, Nature at intervals drops that monstrosity – the killer, a person who slays deliberately, passionlessly."

The road from Fort Scott to Independence, Kansas, cut across the northwest corner of Labette County into Montgomery County. On that little strip of land in Labette County, the Benders, a family of four, settled in the summer of 1871. They were five miles northeast of the nearest town, Cherryvale, in Montgomery County.

They had no close neighbors and they were not overly friendly to those who did come to see them. To say the least, they were an odd family. The father was a huge, broad-shouldered man with piercing black eyes and bushy eyebrows. He was tall but walked slumped forward and reminded some neighbors of a gorilla.

The woman was about the same age as the man, approximately sixty years old, fat and also slumped over, her droopy eyelids hiding a hatred of the world around her.

Their son, John, about twenty-five years old, could make a nice appearance if he chose. But he had a nervous laugh that accompanied everything he said and some thought he was feeble-minded.

The memorable one of the family was the daughter, Kate. She was a couple of years younger than John, of average height and weight. Few people who met her noticed anything other than her bright flashing hazel eyes and her flaming copper-colored hair. There wasn't a young man in the neighborhood who didn't think she was a "looker." Unlike the rest of the family, she talked a lot and was a good mixer. No one would suspect anything much out of the ordinary about the family while Kate was around.

In the first months they were there, the Benders built a small sod house and barn and planted an orchard of about fifty fruit trees, which they cultivated and cared for attentively. They seemed to be like any ordinary homestead family. They stocked a few non-perishable foods and put out a sign that said, "Groceries." Since they were far from any town on a road that was well traveled, they attracted a variety of visitors.

The house had only one room but there was a long curtain in the center that reached from wall to wall and touched the floor. It divided the front room, where visitors and customers were welcomed, and the living quarters, which were behind the curtain. They advertised food and coaxed people to stop and eat.

There was an eerie atmosphere about the place that some people didn't like. But those were local people and the Benders gave the neighbors no trouble. The family was marked off as just a queer bunch of German people.

What the neighbors didn't see was what made the Benders a family to be reckoned with. It was the offer to furnish a reasonably priced meal for the passing travelers that brought the people to the house. If there was more than one person, the travelers were treated courteously, fed, and sent on their way. It was the lone traveler that the Benders longed to see.

There were many men riding along the road by themselves and when one of them stopped in, the Bender household began to bustle. Maybe it was the money that most travelers carried that the Benders wanted.

But money appeared to be a side issue to their main attraction. They loved to kill.

Kate Bender was the leader of the four. Some decided later that they might not even have been a family. Maybe they were just four criminals who had banded together to accomplish their gruesome work. It was Kate who masterminded the insidious scheme. The others moved at her command. She brought in the customers; she set the trap; she ordered it sprung. She might even have done the killing, too, but the old man usually delivered the initial blow. He was the strongest and somebody had to keep the victim's attention away from him. None of them could do that better than Kate.

She coaxed the stranger in for a meal and the old lady got the food ready. The table was behind the curtain with the stove and beds. She sat the stranger at the table with his back to the curtain. The victim usually preferred that spot because he would be facing those in the room. But if he leaned back, his head pressed against the curtain. It made a target the old man with the big hammer couldn't miss.

After the old man had delivered his blow, which likely killed the man, someone cut his throat. Likely Kate did that job. Then the corpse was robbed and partly disrobed.

Getting rid of the body was the next chore. They had that figured exactly. There was a trap door in the floor of the kitchen. If there was any danger of anyone else showing up or if it was daylight when the killing took place, they simply opened the trap door and shoved the corpse into the pit below. Then when night came, they dragged the body out to the orchard and buried it.

People thought the Benders were good workers because they cultivated and harrowed their orchard almost daily. The night orchard burials would never be noticed after the ground was thoroughly harrowed the next morning.

The Benders used the pit often. If some other traveler turned into their lane or if a neighbor stopped to make some small purchase, they had to get rid of the body quickly. If there happened to be some blood around, it could easily be passed off as blood from a chicken or pig they had killed.

The two older Benders and John were surly people and their surliness discouraged any neighbor who felt it was his duty to be friendly. They made it clear they preferred to be left alone and, after an encounter with the older Benders, visitors made sure they got their wish.

Kate claimed to have the gift of second sight and spiritualism and gave seances. It was another way to attract visitors, some of whom might excite her lust to kill. But most of those who were intrigued with Kate's seances were local people. And Kate, in charge of the four Benders, kept her goal of dealing only with travelers who were passing through. The disappearance of a local person would surely stir up a search that could explode the scheme.

Now and then a letter came from the east asking for information about a relative who had been traced out of Fort Scott and across Bourbon County, the corner of Crawford County, and well into Neosho County. Then it was lost as it tipped through the northwest corner of Labette County and was not found at all in Montgomery County. Having those trails disappear made the residents of northwest Labette County nervous. What was happening to those men?

Stories began to surface about some weird happenings, but nothing that pointed to the Benders. They were just a family to be left alone as much as possible.

One story would have alarmed everyone if it had happened to anyone but a very odd

View of early
Independence, Kansas.

Kansas State Historical Society

lady named Hesler. She was called eccentric and that was being very generous. She was into spiritualism and seances and gravitated to Kate Bender. She went to Bender's little house one evening for a seance. Kate wasn't really in the mood. Hesler, who carried a shotgun everywhere she went and declared she was afraid of nothing, told a story the next day that didn't fit her character.

Hesler said she was having a nice visit until about sundown. Then the family began acting weird. They drew pictures of men on the wall and threw knives at the pictures. Kate led the action and told her visitor that the spirits were telling her to kill. Hesler reported that Kate's face changed into a horror mask and she came toward her saying that the spirits were telling her to "kill you – kill you – now!"

Hesler was an old lady not known for her speed. But she flew out of the Bender house and on home where she got inside and locked the door. The story would have upset the listeners except for the fact that everyone knew that Hesler was "off her rocker" and she apparently had yielded to her wild imagination.

There was another unsettling occurrence that couldn't be so easily dismissed. This time it involved a priest, Father Ponziglione. He was traveling through the country and saw the Bender house just at dusk and a rainstorm was coming up. He turned in, expecting to stay the night. The air was close and charged. He laid it to the coming storm but it made him extremely uneasy. He felt that some disaster was about to happen.

Kate was talking to him and laughing at every little joke she told. But he couldn't rid himself of the awful apprehension that gripped him. It didn't ease any when he saw old Mr. Bender take a heavy iron hammer and place it on the other side of the curtain that divided the room. The storm hit and thunder rolled. The priest remembered some of the frightening stories he had heard about people disappearing in this area.

At a loud clap of thunder, he jumped to his feet, saying something about seeing to his horse, and ran out. He jerked up the cinch on the saddle, leaped aboard, and charged out of the yard. Later, when the mystery had been solved, he was certain, and others concurred, that he had been marked for the sacrifice that night but had dashed away just in time.

The people of the community were beginning to look about them. Too many men had disappeared close enough that it was time to begin asking questions of neighbors. Still, the Benders were under no real suspicion.

Then a prime victim came one evening to the Bender home. A Doctor York from Independence was coming home from Fort Scott where he had been visiting relatives. Night overtook him just as he was passing the Bender house. It was still a long way to Independence. even five miles to Cherryville was too far to ride, as tired as he was. So he turned in.

The Benders didn't know York, but they understood he was a doctor and doctors usually had money. He was the perfect victim. The Benders loved killing just for the thrill of killing. But if they could get money along with the killing, it would help to buy what they had to have to run their little store.

They followed the same pattern that had been so successful in the past. Before Doctor York could eat his supper, he was hit in the head with the iron hammer, crushing his skull. They dumped him into the pit to wait until about midnight. Then they took him out, took his money, rings, and anything else of value. Like the rest of the victims, he was buried in the orchard.

In their excitement at landing such a prime victim, the Benders neglected to find out where he was from. If they had known he was from Independence, they might have curbed their excitement. Independence was only ten or twelve miles south. Even more important was something that they couldn't have known. Doctor York had a brother who had once been a member of the Kansas legislature and was known for his bulldog tenacity. He would find his lost brother if it

was possible. And he had the resources to finance the search.

Within a week after Doctor York was reported missing, Colonel York, his brother, was on his trail. It didn't take long to trace him by people who had seen him as far as the area close to the Montgomery – Labette County line. The last person he found who had seen Doctor York was on a farm just a couple of miles from Bender homestead.

Colonel York went to the Benders to ask questions. Kate answered as she always did. She said that Doctor York had been there, watered his horse, and rode on. Kate told Colonel York that she was clairvoyant and, given a chance, could find Doctor York. But she couldn't get into the mood that night. She asked him to come back the next morning and he said he would. There is no record showing that he did.

A few days later, an item in the newspaper said a team and wagon had been found at Thayer, several miles north and east in Neosho County. A quick trip there told investigators that the wagon and team belonged to the Benders. The depot agent said four people had bought tickets on the train to Humboldt. But that had been some time ago. Some men positively identified the team and wagon as belonging to the Benders.

The rumor that the Benders had all been murdered, the latest in the string of murders in the area, was squelched when word spread around that the Benders had apparently left the country.

There was a crowd at Bender's house when the neighborhood men began to search for clues to their disappearance. The trap door was found and the pit uncovered. The foul odor coming from the pit was almost unbearable. The blood clotted on the stones in the bottom of the pit told them the whole story. They had finally identified the murderers who had terrified the area.

Kansas State Historical Society
Cowboy statue on Boot Hill

care of their orchard, harrowing it almost every day.

The first grave they opened was that of Doctor York. They found many more, mostly near the little trees. Off to one side of the orchard they found another grave of a man and a small girl about five years old. She had apparently been killed with her father.

Such a sensational story could not be allowed to die. The villains had escaped and the general public could not tolerate that. There were rumors the Benders had been seen here or there. Some over-zealous self-appointed detectives even brought in people they accused of being the Benders. But it was always easy to prove that they were not.

Some stories said a posse that had gone out to find the Benders had succeeded. The killers allegedly were hanged and thrown in the river, weighted down with rocks. One fantastic story told by a sea captain declared that the gondola of a balloon had crashed on the deck of his ship. The survivor, John Bender, told a wild story of how the Benders had found a hot steam vent and had filled their balloon with hot air and were on their way to South America when the balloon burst and he had landed on the ship. As one great teacher said: "There is no harm in telling a lie so big that nobody can believe it."

Then began the search for the bodies. There were no signs of graves until someone thought of the orchard. It had been over two weeks since the last grave had been put there and no harrowing had been done. The ground had dried out, leaving cracks in the shape of large rectangles. Now they understood why the Benders had taken such good

One popular story was that Colonel York had gone back to the Bender house the next morning after talking to Kate. There he killed all the Benders. To cover up his deed, he had driven the Benders' old wagon to Thayer, dressed two of his men as women, and bought four tickets to Humboldt. People would believe that the Benders had escaped and nobody would ever know that Colonel York and three of his men had killed the family. That story doesn't make much sense but it may have been comforting for people to believe the Benders paid the price for their murderous deeds.

Dodge City: Cow Town
Ford County — 1872-1876

Dodge City was the last of the Kansas cattle shipping towns. It was also the wildest with the most killings. The town sprang into being as soon as the railroad reached the area. It was the farthest west of any town that provided a market for Texas cattle. The towns to the east had put a stop to the cattle coming up the trail. Farmers were putting up fences and threatening to shoot any critter that tried to come through.

The towns were getting weary of the turbulence stirred up by the cowboys coming off a two- or three-month trail drive. The citizens who had welcomed the business when the trail herds first came realized that the damage to the town's growth far outweighed the amount of cash that flowed in from the pleasure seeking cowboys.

Dodge City could see what had happened to the cattle towns in eastern Kansas. Even the most optimistic realized the good times would not last forever in Dodge, either. But while it did last, there wasn't a merchant who didn't try to get as much of that cowboy money as possible.

At the town's inception, it wasn't cattle that brought in the most money It was the buffalo hunters who piled their hides beside the tracks to be loaded on cars and hauled east. Some of the more elite of the town thought the hunters brought more stink than cash because the smell of the hides was carried by the breezes to every corner of the town.

Then came the cattle with a different odor. It was more endurable than the smell of the hides but the buffalo hunter had more money than the cowboy. Often the hunter could earn as much as a hundred dollars in a day. That was three or four months' wages for the trail driver. Both hunters and drovers spent their wages recklessly. And often, after too much drinking, they spent their lives just as carelessly.

A shave, a drink of whiskey, or a box of matches cost the same, twenty-five cents. Nobody gave a thought to the fact that in most places, a shave was ten cents and a box of matches was a nickel. Money, whiskey, and wild women were all plentiful, and to the hunter and trail driver, all three were the epitome of the good life. They went after their shares.

Add to the cowboys and the hunters, the mule skinners and bullwhackers who had been traveling the Santa Fe Trail for years before Dodge City existed, and the soldiers from Fort Dodge, only five miles away, and the town had a mix that was as explosive as gunpowder and matches.

In its first year of existence, Dodge City put fourteen men with slow guns in the new cemetery on the hill. The cemetery earned the name of Boot Hill because most of its residents died with their boots on.

There were two factions in the milling population of the town. There was the "inner" group, made up of the people who lived in town, and the "outer" group, composed of the hunters, cowboys, freighters and soldiers, plus a few residents who deemed the town unfit to live in and put their dugouts beyond the city limits. A majority of the conflicts that erupted within the town involved those groups. Those conflicts added to the population of Boot Hill at an alarming rate.

The buffalo hunter made the most money and looked down his nose at anyone who worked for wages. The mule skinner and bullwhacker had traveled the dangerous road so long that he felt superior to any greenhorn who had just come to town. The soldier was a professional and he wasn't about to take a back seat to anybody who thought he was better with a gun.

To put an end to the carnage, the town officials hired the best gunmen in the country to establish law and order. For a while, these men seemed only to add to the slaughter as they used their own weapons to settle quarrels. But eventually, the cowboy, who got his courage from the bottle, realized the futility of opposing the professional gunmen and sneaked his horse and his gun back to camp. The other would-be kings of the hill got the same message and shied away from the men with the fast guns. Only then did Dodge City begin to settle down.

But it had to travel many bloody miles to reach that point.

Murdered by Vigilantes
Ford County — 1873

Since Dodge City was too far out on the prairie to be under the jurisdiction of an organized county, it had no official government, not even a city marshal. It was the ideal place for some of the worst of the bad men. The core of the town's business section was not of the outlaw element but the merchants had no legal protection.

They turned to the only alternative left to them. They formed a vigilance committee. For a while, that worked wonders. There were enough members of the committee to run out any undesirable resident who was causing trouble.

But as more undesirables moved into Dodge, they began to defy the vigilantes. The vigilantes decided to bolster their ranks with some men who were as good with their guns as the transient gunmen. It appeared to work for a short time. But the new vigilantes soon became as rough as the outlaws they were supposed to control.

The original vigilantes were helpless to straighten things out. They couldn't kick out the undesirable members even though they outnumbered them on the committee. Since every member of the vigilance committee was sworn to secrecy, no member dared speak out against the group or any member.

But the drop of water that broke the dam came when two members of the committee, out to strike a personal blow, killed a harmless Negro soldier named Taylor.

Taylor was serving the commanding officer of Fort Dodge and had been sent to town for some supplies. He left the team and hack in front of a store while he made his purchases. Some roughnecks, members of the vigilance committee, grabbed the hack and drove away.

Taylor dashed out of the store and ran after the hack. He was responsible for the safety of the team and wagon. The two men in the hack deliberately shot Taylor and killed him.

The other vigilantes didn't know what the two men, Scott and Hicks, had against Taylor. Perhaps their disagreement was with the commanding officer of the fort. But it struck the honest vigilantes crosswise to have to tolerate the murder of Taylor.

It was June 3, 1873, and the tempers in the fort erupted. According to one report, a company of Negro soldiers started toward town to burn the place to the ground. They said the government was determined to get rid of the town that was giving the fort so much trouble. But Tom Nixon, who would show up later in the history of Dodge City, organized forty buffalo hunters and moved out to face the troops. Those forty "Big 50" Sharps rifles were enough to send the little army back to the fort.

By telegraph, the commanding officer got a warrant to search the town for the killers of Taylor. He sent a major and some cavalry to town and blocked off the streets so no one could escape. The soldiers searched the town. They found one man who said that he had witnessed an unusual event right after the killing. Someone had thrown a blanket over Taylor's body and one man, Hicks, had lifted the blanket and pointed to one bullet hole and said, "I shot him there."

The soldiers found Hicks and arrested him. The other man, Scott, hid in an ice box in Peacock's Saloon until night then made his escape.

Vigilance committees played an important part on the frontier before legal authority arrived. But they had to be controlled by rational men to be effective.

McCluskie-Anderson Fight
Barber County — June 1873

Hugh Anderson, who killed Mike McCluskie in Newton in 1871, had a job as bartender in Harding's Trading Post in Medicine Lodge in June 1873. Mike's brother, Art McCluskie, vowed vengeance for his brother's death and went looking for Anderson. He located him in Medicine Lodge and challenged him to a battle to the death.

McCluskie didn't follow the pattern of revenge killing where the avenger shot the murderer on the spot without threat or challenge.

One reporter gave a very colorful description of the battle in all its gruesome glory but even he didn't explain why McCluskie challenged Anderson instead of assassinating him. Perhaps he wanted to make Anderson suffer the way Mike McCluskie had suffered when Anderson murdered him.

Art McCluskie even went so far as to give Anderson his choice of weapons. When Anderson received the challenge, he accepted immediately. Apparently he was sure he

Kansas State Historical Society

C. B. Whitney, sheriff of Ellsworth County

could handle McCluskie as easily as he had his brother. Anderson, being smaller than McCluskie, chose guns rather than knives.

They picked Harding, Anderson's employer, as referee. Harding took the two gladiators out in front of his establishment and placed them twenty paces apart, backs to each other, guns in hand.

It was to be a fight to the death with no interference from anyone, regardless of what happened. Harding didn't count to three. One or both of the men would likely have jumped the gun. He simply said, "Now!"

Both men whirled and fired. Both missed, evidently shooting as they turned instead of zeroing in on their targets. It was McCluskie who drew first blood. His second shot hit Anderson in the arm, knocking him to the ground.

The shooting of Sheriff Whitney

From his knees, Anderson fired again. This shot hit McCluskie in the face, ripping away part of his jaw. McCluskie screamed, more from rage than pain, and lunged forward.

Anderson had the advantage now and he waited a second for the big man to get closer, then he fired twice, hitting McCluskie in the belly and in the shoulder. McCluskie went down and the onlookers thought the fight was over.

But McCluskie's rage would not let him die without a final effort. He struggled to raise his gun and fired one last shot, hitting Anderson in the belly.

McCluskie had to know that his time was short. But he pulled out his knife and painfully dragged himself a few feet closer to Anderson. People begged Harding to stop the fight. But Harding had agreed it was to be a fight to the finish. As long as both men had breath, it wasn't over.

Anderson watched McCluskie creep closer to him. He rolled on his side and pulled out his own knife. When McCluskie got near enough, Anderson lunged with his knife, driving the blade into the big man's neck. With life gurgling out of him, McCluskie summoned his last ounce of strength and lunged forward, driving his knife into Anderson's side. The two died together in a giant pool of blood.

Sheriff Whitney Killed
Ellsworth County — August, 1872

Chauncey Whitney had been with Colonel Forsyth at the Battle of Beecher Island on the Arikaree River in northeastern Colorado in September of 1868. He spent nine days in that siege so there wasn't much that he was afraid of any more.

He was elected sheriff of Ellsworth County and his office was in Ellsworth. The town had its own policemen but at times, Whitney had to help out. Most of the crimes committed in the county occurred in Ellsworth. The cattle drives farther east had been blocked off by farmers and Ellsworth became a good place to bring the Texas herds. It was a busy summer in 1872.

Ben Thompson, the noted gunman, had tried to sell his Bull's Head Saloon in Abilene. But with the cattle market gone, so was any interest in Ben's establishment. Broke and angry, Ben and his brother, Billy, turned to Ellsworth, where the action had gone. They found a town seething with unrest and anger. The cattle market had dropped and the Texas cattlemen were finding it hard to sell enough cattle to pay off the drovers.

Ben Thompson opened a gambling room in one of the saloons and got into the business he knew best. But the cowboys didn't have as much money as usual and their fun was cut short. Their tempers were even shorter. Quarrels were frequent and fights were breaking out in many spots. One reporter sent word back to his paper that "Hell is still in session in Ellsworth."

The seeds of trouble were sown right where people should have expected it – Ben Thompson's gambling table. A man named John Sterling got into a game at Thompson's request, to cover a large bet one man insisted on making. Sterling was half drunk but he told Ben that he would give him half of his winnings if he got any.

The game went Sterling's way and he did win a lot of money. But he left without giving Ben his share. Ben Thompson found Sterling later and asked for his money. Guns were banned in town. Sterling knew that and he slapped Ben Thompson instead of paying him. He was positive that Ben didn't have a gun. Nobody slapped Ben Thompson and lived to tell about it.

Thompson was unarmed but he made for Sterling, bare-handed. However, Sterling had a good friend with him, Jack Morco, one of the policemen of Ellsworth. He was armed, of course, so Ben had to back down.

Ben Thompson wasn't about to forget that slap in the face. He would look for Sterling when he got his gun. But Ben was challenged before he could get his weapon. It was Sterling and Morco who yelled for Ben to come out of his gambling room. Ben made a dash into the saloon where the guns had been checked for the day.

Billy Thompson, drunk as usual, decided to join his brother. When Ben grabbed his revolver and a rifle, Billy got Ben's shotgun. They ran back to the place where the two gunmen had challenged Ben but they were already gone.

Russell Springs, Kansas
Butterfield Trail Historical Society Photos

Barn where outlaws holed up.

Ben yelled for Sterling and Morco to come out. They didn't respond but Sheriff Whitney heard the commotion and came out to quiet things down. He appeared to have things under control and they went back into the saloon. Billy Thompson took the lead, carrying the shotgun, fully cocked. He thought he needed another drink.

Ben was warned suddenly by a friend that Sterling was coming for him. Ben rushed back outside and dived into an alley. Sterling saw him and he plunged into a doorway. Ben shot at him and missed. Some said it was the first time Ben Thompson ever missed a target.

Sheriff Whitney rushed outside to stop the shooting. Hearing the shot that Ben had fired, Billy turned toward the door and staggered into the street, the shotgun still cradled loosely in his hands.

Hays City, Kansas, 1871

Ellis County Historical Society

What happened next is still unclear. What is clear is that Billy's shotgun went off, the charge hitting Whitney in the back, puncturing a lung and his shoulder.

Some said it was an accident; others thought that Billy just saw somebody ahead of him and fired, too drunk to know or care what he hit. Mayor Miller demanded that his policemen disarm Ben Thompson and Sterling. None of the policemen would face Ben Thompson and demand his gun. The mayor fired them all.

The shooting of Sheriff Whitney, who was a favorite of everybody, especially the Thompsons, put a damper on the original fight between Sterling and Ben Thompson. A truce was struck and the guns were put away.

Ben was furious with his brother and drove him out of town. The fighting was over. But Chauncey Whitney, everybody's friend, died three days later.

Life was cheap in early Kansas days.

Killers at Russell Springs
Logan, Kingman Counties — 1874

Two men, one nineteen and the other an older hardened criminal, got into serious trouble in Kingman, Kansas.

The marshal in Kingman tried to arrest them but they stood their ground and used their guns. They killed the marshal, then fled.

After they left Kingman, the fugitives showed up in Dighton. Perhaps to show how mean they were, they caught an old man and tied him to a manger in the livery barn, blindfolded him, then made him eat hay. They apparently thought it was a great joke.

They left the old man tied up and headed northwest. Obviously, they felt that they were far ahead of any pursuit. But the old man got loose from the manger in Dighton just in time to meet the posse from Kingman. He felt he had a score to settle with the two and he asked to go along. His request was approved.

The killers arrived in Russell Springs in Logan County just at supper time. They got something to eat and then were invited to attend the literary which was being held that night at the courthouse. The two turned down the invitation, saying they wanted to get an early start the next morning. They would just sleep in the loft of the livery barn.

Perhaps it was that rejection of the invitation to the literary that aroused some suspicion among the people of the little town. Russell Springs, the county seat of Logan County, had a sheriff and a deputy sheriff.

Death Hollow, site of the Indian attack on the German Family.

Author's photo

But they had very little work to do in the way of crime control.

The suspicion was vague. Most travelers were glad to stay in the small hotel in the east part of town. Why did these men choose to stay in the livery barn loft? Albert Hall, who owned and operated the livery barn, had the same question. The two men had never mentioned their names. They were total strangers to the citizens of the town.

One man rode to Oakley, about twenty miles to the northeast, right in the corner of Logan County, and came back before daylight with descriptions of two men who had killed the marshal in Kingman. Those descriptions fit the two men sleeping in the haymow of Albert Hall's livery barn.

Within a short time, men from all around town got their guns and surrounded the barn. They even guarded the roads in case the two managed to slip past the guards.

As soon as it began to get light, Sheriff Bud Perryman and his deputy, Sam Bish, climbed as quietly as possible up the ladder toward the manhole through which hay was thrown down to the horses. With guns drawn, they moved out on the haymow floor toward the hay stored against the side of the haymow. They expected to find the suspects

there because their horses were in the barn below.

It was still too dark under the barn roof to see much. They crept forward until they were able to make out the forms of the two sleeping men. Apparently they had been on the run long enough to be dead tired. The sheriff and his deputy, with their guns pointed directly into the faces of the fugitives, roused the two.

The killers had no chance to escape. The people of Russell Springs, not accustomed to facing murderers, breathed a sigh of relief. Frances Hall, a small girl then, was let out of the pantry where her mother had put her for fear of stray bullets coming through the house if a gun fight developed. Albert Hall's house stood directly north of his livery stable.

The two men, handcuffed, were put in a wagon and, with an escort of men headed back to Kingman where they would go on trial.

The younger of the two, still under-age, was sent to the reformatory and the older one went to the penitentiary in Lansing.

Sophia and Catherine German

Julia and Nancy German

German Family Massacre
Logan County — September 1874

John and Lydia German left Georgia in 1870 with their seven children. One of the older girls, Catherine, could not tolerate the damp southern climate and the parents decided to move the family to the dry plains of eastern Colorado.

They had to stop frequently to find work to earn money for food and clothing. So it was four years before they finally packed up in Chautauqua County, Kansas, for the last leg of their journey.

It was August and they headed northwest, following the railroad past Hays. They were told at Ellis to go south to the old Smoky Hill Trail where they could find water. There would be none along the railroad farther west.

Traveling was easier on the old trail and by September 10, they had reached the forks of the Smoky Hill. They camped there. Two men came down the trail from the west that evening. They told them that it was only fourteen miles to Fort Wallace.

The Germans had an ox team and twelve miles was a big day's travel for them. The family decided they would get an early start and reach the fort the next day.

They were up at dawn. Lydia and the oldest daughter, Rebecca, got breakfast. Then Stephen, the only boy in the family, and Catherine, both in their late teens, went out north to bring in their two cows and their calves. The other four girls, Joanna,

Sophia, Julia and Nancy, the last two born since the war, fed the chickens in the crates.

The oxen were moving up the slope from the campsite when the wild whoops of Indians split the air. John was walking in front. Lydia and Rebecca were on the wagon seat driving. The other four girls were riding in the back of the wagon.

The Indians exploded out of a ravine that paralleled the trail the Germans were following. John jerked up his rifle but an arrow drove through his heart before he could pull the trigger. He fell and Lydia leaped off the wagon seat to run to him. An Indian drove a tomahawk into her skull. Rebecca grabbed an ax standing in the front of the wagon box. She smashed the blade into a warrior's shoulder as he reached to pull her out of the wagon. Another Indian shot her before she could swing the ax again.

There were three dead in less than half a minute. Some of the warriors swarmed around the girls in the back of the wagon. Others headed out where Stephen and Catherine were trying to hide behind a hill.

Since the two were on foot, the warriors soon caught up with them. They killed Stephen instantly. One warrior shot an arrow into Catherine's thigh, knocking her down. He leaped off his pony, pulling out the arrow, then threw her, screaming, onto the horse and leaped on behind her.

Back at the wagon, the warriors were ripping through the things in the trunks, grabbing any trinket that caught their fancy.

The Indians had killed four of the family – the parents and the two oldest children, Rebecca and Stephen. They still had the five youngest girls to deal with. They took the two oldest, Catherine and Joanna, around the wagon and made them take off their bonnets. Although Joanna was almost two years younger than Catherine, she had long

German Family monument in Ft. Wallace Cemetery

Author's photos

The 1990 peace conference between German Family descendants and Cheyennes.

dark hair and Catherine's hair was cut short. They chose Joanna, killed her and scalped her. Her hair made a much nicer scalp than Catherine's.

The three older girls were stunned and silent. But Nancy Adelaide, only five years old, cried and wouldn't stop. One warrior brought up his bow and was going to kill her but one of the two squaws in the group jumped in front of Nancy and stopped the warrior. Then she claimed Nancy and Julia, the two youngest, for her own.

What followed was a nightmare for the four German girls. The two smallest ones with the little squaw who had saved Nancy's life had it easier than the other girls, Catherine and Sophia. Those two were separated and each had to do the work of a squaw. Whenever the warriors were gone on a hunt or to battle, the squaws took great delight in beating the white girls. They bore the marks of those beatings for a long time.

The Indians took their captives southwest to the Staked Plains of the western panhandle of Texas and the eastern plains of New Mexico. The two older girls didn't see the younger sisters since they were taken with a different branch of the tribe. When the Indians saw how much comfort the two older sisters got from each other's company, they separated them, fearing that, together, they might try to escape. Alone, they were not so likely to make an attempt.

The little girls were not getting enough to eat but they were faring better than the older ones who had very short rations and had to work hard besides. They were together again near where Pampa, Texas, stands today, when the Indians suddenly took alarm at something. Evidently a messenger had brought them word of approaching danger. They had been sure they were out of range of any soldiers.

Two Indians took the smaller girls back to their last camp and abandoned them. They were too small to keep up and the Indians had to travel fast to escape the approaching troops.

The approaching soldiers did not find Julia and Nancy. The girls had to forage for themselves. Coming across a spot where the army had camped, they found some grain the horses hadn't eaten and a few scraps that the troopers had thrown away. They survived on those and the few plums they found along the river.

In early November, word reached the chiefs that the army was demanding that they return the four captives immediately or suffer the consequences.

Back in Kansas, a hunter had found the five bodies and the burned wagon of the Germans about two weeks after the massacre. Near the burned wagon, a Bible had somehow escaped the flames. In it was the record of the German family, listing all nine names with birth dates. The authorities knew four were missing and, from the small tracks around the camping area, that some were children.

The search was on. Companies of soldiers were sent over the southwest. It was the approach of some of those troops that sent the Indians scurrying to the northwest. But it was about three weeks before Julia and Nancy were found, again by the Indians. Another threatening message had reached their chief, listing what would happen to them if they did not return the four captives alive and well. Until then, the Indians likely had no idea the army would ever miss the captives, much less know exactly how many were missing. So the chief sent some warriors back to find the little girls they had abandoned. They did find them and started back to the tribe.

On the second day of the return trip, the Indians were surprised by soldiers. Lieutenant Baldwin was searching the north branch of McClellan Creek when a scout raced back to report a band of Indians not far ahead. Baldwin hurried forward until he located the Indians. Knowing that Indians usually killed their captives if they felt they were going to lose a battle, the lieutenant decided on a surprise attack.

With Company D of the 6th Cavalry and Company D of the 5th Cavalry, he charged the camp. The Indians had no time to take care of any details but the battle raged for hours. The Indians never got back to their camp.

Wichita Marshal Mike Meagher, left, and brother
John, in their youth.

Kansas State Historical Society Photos

Wichita's first jail

While the soldiers rested after the battle, an Indian slipped back into the former camp and fired a rifle into a pile of buffalo robes. A soldier shot the Indian then they investigated the pile of robes. They found Julia, unhurt, in the robes and she directed them to Nancy, who was off to one side of the camp trying to start a fire, something she had been ordered to do. She was still working at it, ignoring what was going on around her.

The two little girls almost starved to death before rescue. But the two older ones still had to be taken away from the Indians. All Indian rations were stopped as soon as the army discovered which tribe was holding the captives. It was a hard winter and everyone, Indians and captives, were virtually starving.

General Miles sent word to Stone Calf's village on the Staked Plains of eastern New Mexico that they would get no supplies until they returned the captives. The hard part of the winter was ahead of them.

Stone Calf was ready to strike a bargain with the general. He had Catherine and was willing to return her to the army. But Chief Gray Beard, who had Sophia, wanted to hold out for better terms. The stalling and interchanging of letters lasted until February. The Indians were in desperate straits and even Gray Beard knew that many of his tribe would die if they didn't surrender.

The Indians finally sent word they were coming in to surrender and would bring the captives. It took them a long time to get there, due partly to weakened horses and people. But they may also have been hoping going slow would get them better terms. It didn't.

The Indians surrendered at Fort Sill in Oklahoma Territory. The officers wanted Catherine to point out the warriors who took part in the massacre of her family. She saw several but they were not to be found the next morning when the final count was made.

It was difficult to determine what Indian was in charge of the warriors who murdered the Germans. Kicking Horse was listed in some histories and it was quite widely accepted that he was the leader of that raid.

In 1990, the Cheyenne descendants of the participants in the massacre and the descendants of the four German girls who survived, got together on the site of the tragedy and smoked the peace pipe. The Indians were the descendants of Medicine Water, not Kicking Horse. It was Medicine Water who led the ambush on the German family.

It took almost 120 years to establish peace between the two families. But the guns and the tomahawks were laid to rest there on the prairie at the forks of the Smoky Hill River on that September afternoon in 1990.

Meagher-Powell Battle
Sedgwick County — 1877

It was an unusual way to celebrate New Year's Day. Mike Meagher, city marshal of Wichita, was hoping for a quiet holiday that January 1, 1877. And it seemed to be just that except for the theft of a horse. The unexpected part was that the man who stole the horse, Sylvester Powell, was not very smart. He stole the horse from the town's hitch rack in broad daylight within sight of the owner.

The owner objected strenuously and rushed out to claim his horse. Powell dared him to come and take it. The rancher was not a gunfighter and he recognized that Powell was so he backed off.

Author's photo

Castle Rock, southeast of Park, Kansas

He went to the marshal and told Meagher what had happened. He needed his horse and wanted him back.

Meagher went in search of Powell and found him still in town. Meagher arrested Powell and threw him in jail. He gave the horse back to the rightful owner and thought that was the end of the affair.

It wasn't. Sylvester Powell's boss was in town and he went down to the jail and paid the bail to get Powell released. Powell went looking for the marshal who, in his opinion, had wronged him by locking him up. On his way, he stopped at a couple of saloons to bolster his courage.

If he had not been liquored up, Powell likely would not have done what he did when he found the marshal. He discovered that Meagher was behind Hope's Saloon, sitting in the outhouse. He didn't wait for Meagher to come out. He opened fire through the side of the building.

Clay Allison

Kansas State Historical Society Photos

Wyatt Earp

One shot ripped a hole in Meagher's coat and another shot hit him in the leg. Powell was sure he had killed the lawman so he went back to the street to decide which saloon was worthy of his celebration.

Meagher was anything but dead. He was, however, as mad as a bull. After he got presentable, he went looking for the would-be assassin. He found Powell standing in front of Hill's Drug Store. From the careless way he stood there surveying the saloons along the street, it was obvious that he was sure Meagher was dead or injured so seriously that he'd be unable to come after him.

Still seething, Meagher wasn't even polite enough to notify Powell of his mistaken assumption. He took careful aim and shot Powell through the heart. The number of horse thieves roaming the streets of Wichita was reduced by one.

End of the Track
for Train Robbers
Gove County — 1877

Tiny Buffalo Park or Buffalo Station (today's Park, Kansas) seemed like a very unlikely place for outlaws. But two train robbers were there one foggy September morning in 1877.

To find the reason for their presence there, go back to Big Springs, Nebraska, a few days prior to their stop in Buffalo Park. Sam Bass got the credit for master-minding that train robbery at Big Springs. He had five men with him, including Joel Collins and Bill Heffridge.

The robbery was carefully planned. The six outlaws rode up to the station about 10 o'clock at night. They forced the agent, George Barnhart, to shut down his telegraph and put out the red light to tell the engineer to stop the train.

The train came through a few minutes before eleven and stopped as the red light demanded. Under six guns, the engineer, train crew and passengers could do little but comply with the orders of the outlaws.

The combination lock on the big safe could not be opened but the bandits found three boxes of freshly minted gold coins, each box reported to contain twenty thousand dollars.

They weren't satisfied with that and went through the train, forcing passengers to hand over their money and jewelry. Then the far-off whistle of another approaching train forced them to load their loot and ride away to the south as fast as the horses could go.

They split up into three pairs, each going in different directions. Collins and Heffridge teamed up to go southeast, aiming for Missouri. That was how they happened to pass through Buffalo Park that foggy morning.

Such a huge robbery was big news and the story was spread far and wide. Scanty descriptions of the men were given; names were used if they happened to be known. Fortune hunters to the south of Big Springs were on the lookout for the robbers. Many were not looking for a reward but hoping they could catch them, relieve them of their gold, and never report that the thieves had come their way.

Someone saw Heffridge and Collins crossing the Nebraska – Kansas state line, heading south and reported the sighting to officials. Word was sent on ahead in the direction the two seemed to be headed. Hays, Kansas was one of the places alerted. The sheriff of Ellis County took ten soldiers from Fort Hays and went up the tracks to the area where they expected the two robbers to cross the railroad.

They guessed exactly right. The only thing that they hadn't prepared for was the fog that early morning. The outlaws didn't see the little camp of soldiers close to the tracks and the soldiers didn't see the outlaws.

One reason the robbers came to Buffalo Park was to get something to eat where they would be least likely to run into any trouble. They asked the telegraph operator, Bill Sternberg, where they could get supplies. He took them up to Thompson's section house. There he noticed an envelope in one of their pockets with the name Collins on it. He had read the names of the known outlaws in the paper and Collins was one of them.

As soon as the men rode on, the telegrapher notified the soldiers and they went after the pair. They caught them a short distance from the station. The two didn't seem alarmed. When the Ellis County sheriff asked them to come back to the station and identify themselves, they agreed. They said they had helped drive a herd of cattle north and were now going back to Texas. That looked suspicious to the sheriff and the soldiers. The two would have to turn almost straight south to hit Texas and they were holding to a southeasterly course.

They started back calmly. Then suddenly both Heffridge and Collins went for their guns. But the soldiers had been expecting that and they blasted them both out of their saddles.

They were the first of the six robbers to pay the supreme price for their folly and the only ones to die in Kansas.

Earp, Allison Showdown
Ford County — 1877

When Mayor Hoover hired Wyatt Earp to head up the deputies in Dodge City, his instructions to Earp were to keep an iron hand on things but not to kill unless absolutely necessary. Wyatt hired three deputies. One was Joe Mason, who had been a deputy under the previous marshal. The other two were the Masterson brothers, Bat and Jim.

The four men did a good job of following Mayor Hoover's orders. If things didn't get too wild south of the tracks, they didn't bother the merry-makers. But when the activity came north of the tracks, heads were cracked on the slightest provocation. The deputies seldom used their guns for anything other than a slap over the head to subdue some law breaker.

Being clubbed over the head and dragged to the jail was very humiliating to the average cowboy who considered himself cock of the walk when he got into a strange town. But shooting deaths in Dodge City declined. The trips to Boot Hill were not as frequent.

There were those who resented the strict enforcement of the law and they took steps to change things. Word came to Dodge City that Clay Allison was coming and he would straighten things out. He thought highly of himself and he had made it clear that nobody, certainly not Wyatt Earp, was going to make him pull in his horns.

Clay Allison had made quite a name for himself. He had killed the city marshals of Cimarron, New Mexico, and Las Animas, Colorado. Both times he had been acquitted on the grounds of self defense. He had been in Dodge City before. One of his victims was buried on Boot Hill. He made it known he was coming to Dodge City for the express purpose of freeing the town of its city marshal.

Wyatt Earp patrolled the streets of Dodge City every night until four in the morning. Then he slept until nearly noon. Allison's arrival was in the early hours of the day. He immediately began touring the saloons, bragging about how he was going to rid the town of Earp.

Earp didn't hear about it until Mayor Hoover woke him up sometime in the forenoon to tell him that Allison was there and making the rounds of the saloons, drinking and bragging. What was he going to do about it?

Wyatt told the mayor to spread the word that he'd be right out to see Allison. Then he took his time shaving and getting a good breakfast. Allison, already half drunk, a condition when he was most dangerous, had to wait, something he didn't do well.

The marshal knew Allison would spend a lot of his fighting energy in talk about what he was going to do. The longer Earp made him wait, the more nervous Allison would get and the less bravado he'd have.

Allison was not popular in Dodge City so Earp had plenty of offers of help in handling him. But he refused any aid other than assigning two of his deputies to guard against an ambush by Allison's friends.

It was 10 o'clock when Wyatt finally started down Front Street. Allison came out of Wright and Beverley's establishment and moved toward Earp.

Earp stopped in front of the Long Branch Saloon and leaned against the wall. Allison stopped only a foot or two from him and pretended that he wasn't sure who he was. His foolish questions were his excuse to get very close to the marshal. Allison kept his right side and hand turned away from Earp while he worked his hand down to his gun.

Earp knew what Allison was trying to do. He was close enough to Allison to feel his muscles tense as he reached for his gun.

Chalk Beeson, in the doorway of the Long Branch, said he saw the snarl on Allison's face as he reached for his gun and, in a split second, that snarl was replaced by a gasp of astonishment. Clay's gun was only half out of the holster when Wyatt poked his pistol into his opponent's left side.

The marshal didn't say a word and, for a moment, Allison didn't, either. Earp waited,

Santa Fe Depot at
Kinsley, Kansas.

not moving. Finally Allison said in a voice that quivered slightly, "I'm going around the corner."

Wyatt told him to go ahead. "Just don't come back."

Allison backed around the corner and Wyatt moved over to look down Second Avenue. Allison was nowhere in sight. From across the street where he had been watching for any sign of an ambush, Bat Masterson called to Wyatt that Allison had gone into Wright and Beverley's by a side door. To Wyatt, that meant more liquor to fortify his ego then he'd likely make another move.

Wyatt stayed at his post in front of the Long Branch. Allison's horse was tied to the hitchrack in front of the saloon. He'd have to come past Wyatt to get his horse before he could leave town – if he had any intention of leaving.

The doors of the Long Branch swung out and Chalk Beeson shoved a shotgun at Wyatt. "Give him both barrels," Beeson advised.

Wyatt refused the offer. "Allison has only two six-guns," he said.

Allison strode out of Wright and Beverley's and walked straight to his horse. Once in the saddle, he turned to Wyatt and demanded that he come over so he could talk to him.

"I can hear you from here," Earp said, not moving.

Allison suddenly found that he had nothing to say. He wheeled his horse and rode to the toll bridge. There he stopped and spun around, facing the plaza. Suddenly he jerked out one gun, put spurs to his horse and, with a wild yell, headed back for the Long Branch.

"Watch the streets!" Wyatt yelled at Bat. "I'm going to get him!"

Earp moved out into the middle of the street, facing the oncoming rider. When Allison was within fifty yards of Wyatt, the marshal lifted his gun out of its holster. Suddenly Allison yanked back on the reins and the horse made a sliding stop. Allison wheeled the horse and dashed back toward the bridge with all the speed he had used in coming. This time he kept right on going out of town.

Marshal Wyatt Earp was still in charge of Dodge City.

Kinsley Train Robbery
Edwards County —
January 27, 1878

Sometimes when things start to go wrong, everything goes the same way. That seemed to be the pattern of the attempted train robbery at Kinsley, Kansas, northeast of Dodge City.

Six men made careful plans to rob the train at the water tank east of Kinsley. They were in for a series of frustrations. The first came when the train did not stop for water. It had taken on water in Dodge City and didn't needed any more.

But the robbers weren't discouraged. They decided to wait for the next train. Any train was almost sure to carry plenty of money.

They rode back west to the station at Kinsley, determined to rob the station itself if they couldn't snare a train. They went inside the station and found Andrew Kinkaide, the night operator. They put a gun in Kinkaide's face and demanded money. Kinkaide said there was no money in the safe and, even if there was, he had no way of opening it.

Kinkaide knew there was a packet of two thousand dollars in the safe but, although facing the robbers' guns, he insisted there was none. Just what the robbers would have done next was sidetracked when a train whistle sounded to the east. The westbound express was coming, that would likely have more money on it than the train they had originally tried to rob.

They pushed Kinkaide out on the platform to wait for the train to stop. Kinkaide broke away and tried to warn the engineer of the trap. He got across the tracks with

Edward (Ed) Masterson

Kansas State Historical Society Photos

William (Bat) Masterson

only one shot being fired at him. That shot startled the brakeman and, before he could get the brakes set on all the cars, the train had run on for a hundred yards beyond the station.

Kinkaide, who had taken refuge behind the train, was left exposed to the robbers on the platform. However, they weren't interested in the stationmaster. They were running after the train.

Two robbers jumped up on the engine and ordered the engineer to get the train moving. Apparently they hoped to get out in the country, then stop the train and rob it. But the engineer said he didn't have enough steam built up to start the train again.

The expressman had a large package to unload in Kinsley and had the door open and the package ready to shove out on the platform. He was waiting for the train to back up so he could unload his package when two of the robbers bobbed up right in front of him.

They demanded that he put up his hands. Instead, he threw his lantern out into the night, grabbed his gun and started shooting. It was a lively but unproductive exchange of shots.

The other two robbers had boarded the train to rob the passengers. But when the two who were holding the engineer at gunpoint heard the shooting back in the express car, they rushed back to help their partners. That left the engineer free and he immediately threw the power to the wheels and the train began rolling forward.

The two at the express car were left on the grade beside the train. The others jumped off and all ran for their horses back at the station.

The engineer stopped the train a couple of miles out of Kinsley. Checking everything, he discovered that nobody had been hurt and nothing had been stolen. The robbery attempt was a total failure.

The railroad officials didn't write the incident off, however. They posted a reward of one hundred dollars for the capture of the robbers, "dead or alive."

Bat Masterson was sheriff of Ford County. Although the attempted robbery took place in Edwards County, he was called on to try to capture the robbers. He was as familiar with the country in that area as anyone because he had spent so much time hunting buffalo there.

The outlaws, realizing what a fuss was being made over a robbery that never really happened, split up so they would be harder to find. The identities of the six men were hard to pin down. The leader, Mike Rourke, an outlaw who had been in many scrapes with the law, was definitely identified. The others were lesser lights in the outlaw world.

Bat Masterson and three deputies trailed some of the outlaws down to the mouth of Crooked Creek south of Dodge City about fifty miles. A blizzard hit and they holed up at Harry Lovell's cattle camp.

Bat was sure that the outlaws would have had to find shelter somewhere because of the blizzard. When the storm was over, they might show up at Lovell's camp looking for food. So he laid an ambush and when two of the men did show up, got the drop on them. He had recognized Dave Hudebaugh and Edgar West, two who had been identified as members of the gang.

Some time later, Masterson heard that a couple of gang members had been spotted in a dance hall in Dodge. He got two deputies and went after them. They had left Dodge but the small posse ran them down and captured them without a fight. The two were named Dugan and Green.

That still left Mike Rourke, the leader, the one authorities really wanted to catch, on the loose. Rourke was seen in Dodge City. Masterson got his deputies again and went

Monument in Oberlin Cemetery to victims of 1878 Indian raid.

Kansas Historical Society

after him. Rourke had two companions with him. Bat trailed them to Lovell's cattle camp where he had caught the first pair of robbers. Rourke had been there but had just left.

The posse stuck to Rourke's trail until he passed over into the area known as No Man's Land where there was no law and lawmen had no authority. Masterson had to give up the chase.

It was October when someone turned in Rourke. He was tried, convicted, and sentenced to ten years in prison at hard labor.

Ed Masterson Killed
Ford County — April 9, 1878

April 9, 1878, was a quiet night north of the tracks in Dodge City. But it was seldom quiet south of the tracks. This night was no exception. About 10 o'clock, shots rang out and Ed Masterson, marshal of Dodge City, took a deputy, Nat Haywood, and crossed the tracks to check out the disturbance.

The officers found some cowboys just off the trail from Texas looking for a good time

They were getting out of hand in the Lady Gay Dance Hall. Jack Wagner was on the wrong side of sober and was causing most of the problems.

Ed Masterson called for Wagner's gun and he handed it over without objection. Ed gave the gun to Wagner's boss, A. M. Walker, with instructions not to let the cowboy have his gun back until they left town.

With quiet reestablished, Ed and his deputy went outside. Before they left the area, Ed saw Wagner and his boss coming out of the Lady Gay. Wagner had his gun back in his holster. Ed stepped up and demanded the gun.

Wagner was so drunk that, he balked at handing over the gun. Ed tried to grab the gun and the two got into a lively scuffle. Deputy Haywood moved up to help Masterson and Walker poked a gun in his face and told him to let them settle their differences alone. Haywood ignored the rancher's warning and Walker pulled the trigger. The gun misfired but it convinced Haywood and he turned and ran for help.

Sheriff Bat Masterson, Ed's brother, heard the yelling and scuffling and came on the run. He was within fifteen yards of the two when a gun roared. Ed fell back from Wagner, his shirt on fire from the powder blast of the shot. The gun was held against Ed's side when it discharged.

The sight of Ed's clothing on fire from the shot was enough to make Bat cut loose. He fired four times and they were not wild shots. His first shot hit Wagner in the stomach. Walker was getting into the fight and Bat's next three shots all struck the cattleman, one shot hitting him in the lungs and one shattering his right arm. Within seconds, the battle was over.

Ed Masterson stumbled across to Hoover's Saloon and fell on the floor, his clothes still on fire. The bullet had passed completely through Ed's body. There was no chance he could survive the wound.

As for Wagner who had been scuffling with Ed, Bat's shot had sent him reeling into Peacock's Saloon. There he found someone he knew and asked him to catch him before he fell. The man only pushed him away, telling him he couldn't help him now. Most of the men there had seen him shoot the marshal. Wagner dropped on the floor and lay there until some Texans picked him up and took him to a room where he died the next day. He was buried on Boot Hill.

George Hinkle in Hoover's Saloon yelled to Bat that Ed was dying. Bat rushed to the saloon and was with his brother when he died half an hour after the fight.

Dodge City had lost one of its favorite marshals.

The Last War Whoop Decatur County — September 1878

By 1878, Kansas homesteaders believed it was safe to plow the sod, and produce their crops. They thought

Historical marker detailing the last Indian raid in the state of Kansas.

the Indians wars were over, But they were wrong.

The warring Northern Cheyennes had surrendered. But the government, in all its wisdom, sent the members of the tribe from their home on the Northern Plains to Oklahoma. The climate was too hot and wet. The Cheyennes began dying like flies.

The Indians broke out of their reservation in September and headed back to their homeland, under the leadership of their two head chiefs, Dull Knife and Little Wolf. When the army scouts caught up with them, they told the scouts that they would fight the soldiers to get back to their homeland but they wouldn't fight civilians unless the civilians fought them first.

The civilians did exactly that near Dodge City as the Indians were crossing the Arkansas River. From then on, any white man the Indians saw was in danger.

The soldiers outnumbered the Indians, although the results of the encounters didn't reflect that superiority.

The Indians tried to avoid contact with whites until they reached Sappa Creek in northern Kansas. Three years earlier, on

April 23, 1875, a company of soldiers, commanded by Lieutenant Heneley, had surrounded the Cheyenne village of Bull Hump on Sappa Creek and killed twenty-two Indians, including Bull Hump. To the Cheyenne way of thinking, that attack had to be avenged. But the warriors agreed they would kill only men, no women.

September 30 was a day no one who lived along Sappa Creek, just southwest of the town of Oberlin, would ever forget. Oberlin had changed its name from Westfield two months earlier.

Henry Anthony was a small boy in 1878, but old enough to remember every moment of that day. He wrote his report for his daughter and it was handed on to his granddaughter.

Henry's older brother, Harry, thirteen, was out looking for cattle that morning when the Indians appeared. One came riding toward him and Harry whipped his horse toward home. When he got close to the house, he leaped off his horse and ran inside. The Indian followed him and he grabbed the horse and led it away.

Two neighbors, William Laing and his son, Freeman, were driving along the road near the Anthony house when the Indians poured over the hill. The Indians shot both men, stopped the team, cut away the harness, and led the horses back where others were holding the horses they had gathered along the creek.

The few guns the Anthonys had were distributed among those old enough to shoot and the family waited for developments. The Indians came toward the house, apparently not expecting any resistance. The Anthonys had a visitor at the house, Pat Lynch. He had a gun and he waited by a window. When an Indian passed in front of the window, Lynch shot and killed him.

There were Indians on the roof of the house and all over the yard. When Lynch killed the Indian, the other raiders backed off. Those inside the house had expected them to rush the place and kill them all.

Another wagon appeared on the road, apparently on the way to town. By the time the travelers realized their danger, it was too late. The Anthonys recognized two more of their neighbors, Moses Abernathy and George Walters. The Indians killed them and took their horses.

Still within sight of the Anthony house two more neighbors, William Westfall (Westphal), and his son, Freeman, were killed.

The Indians turned west, killing E. P. Humphrey and wounding John Humphrey so seriously he died shortly afterward.

J. J. Keifer managed to escape the Indians. He gathered up Mrs. Humphrey and a couple of other ladies, including Mrs. Guipe and her baby daughter, Pearl. He found some brush piles and hid the women and himself in one of those piles. The Indians searched the area and Keifer had to choke the baby because it was determined to cry. Any sound would have alerted the Indians. Keifer would release his grip on the baby every time he dared so it could get its breath. The Indians burned several piles of brush but they didn't burn the one hiding Keifer and the women. They all escaped harm.

Mrs. Laing was home when the Indians found her place. She watched in horror as they killed her son in the yard. Then they came inside where she had her two youngest children, six and four years old. The Indians piled the furniture and bedding in the middle of the floor, stripped the two children naked and threw them on top of the pile and prepared to set it ablaze to burn the children alive. Mrs. Laing pleaded with them and they finally relented and threw her and the children out of the house before they started the fire. Mrs. Laing used her petticoats to

Boot Hill Museum — Dodge City
Dora Hand, also known as Fannie Keenan, was killed by a bullet meant for the mayor.

cover the children and ran with them to the Anthony house, knowing her husband had gone that way to town and would be sure to stop there on his way home. The Anthonys had to tell her the terrible truth that her husband was dead.

In all, eighteen men and boys had been killed along the Sappa. Thirteen of the bodies were brought to the Anthony home (the only one in the area not destroyed) to await burial in the cemetery in the northeastern corner of Oberlin.

Those killed in the last Indian raid in Kansas were: William, Freeman and John Laing, Jr.; J. D. Smith, Frederick Hamper, E. P. and John Humphrey, Moses Abernathy, John Hudson, George F. Walters, Marcellus Felt, Ed Miskelly, William Westphal and

William Westphal, Jr., two men named Wright, two others named Hull and Irwin.

The Indians moved on, killing one man in Chase County in southwestern Nebraska, then going on into the Sandhills north of the Platte River. They were captured there, taken to Fort Robinson where they made a break in the dead of winter. A few escaped but many were killed.

Late Night Assassin
Ford County — October 2, 1878

Dodge City was home to a strange mix of characters during the early days. The West was lucky that the recipe was lost and the exact mixture was never repeated.

There were bad men and women in Dodge City who could be, and often were, the picture of grace and kindness. And there were apparently good men and women who could be as vile and black-hearted as the basest of criminals.

And there were some who rose above their reputations. Dora Hand was such a person.

Her working name was Fannie Keenan. She was always ready to offer a helping hand to anyone down and out. Many a Texas cowboy who had squandered every penny of his wages in a night or a week in the dives of Dodge City was given a second chance by Dora. If he had bet and lost his saddle, she might buy it back from the gambler who had won it. He could ride home instead of walk. Some owed their last meal in Dodge City to Dora, who also gave them enough money to buy more food on the way home.

The down-and-out drovers blessed her name. Even the high-and-mighty admitted she was generous and deserved some credit. But they were disgusted by her nighttime occupation.

Dora also had a beautiful singing voice. Her name listed on a program guaranteed a full house for the show.

Her daytime activities began to outweigh even the most severe criticism of the shady side of her life.

The mayor of Dodge City, James "Dog" Kelly, was also one of the owners of a saloon on Front Street called the Alhambra. In the summer of 1878, Kelly got into an argument with a man named James Kennedy and threw him out of the saloon.

Kennedy took sharp exception to the treatment he received from Kelly. He left town but he didn't forget.

Everyone knew Mayor Kelly owned a two room shack behind the hotel where he slept when he stayed overnight in Dodge City. In September, Kelly became sick and finally agreed to spend some time in the hospital. Before he went to the hospital, he rented his little shack to a couple of the girls who entertained along Front Street, Fannie Garretson and Fannie Keenan.

At the beginning of October, James Kennedy returned to Dodge City, bent on revenge against Mayor Kelly. He could not forget the humiliation he had suffered at the hands of the mayor.

Kennedy knew where Mayor Kelly slept when he stayed in Dodge City. About four thirty in the morning, Kennedy rode into town. He wanted to be sure that no one saw him and he also wanted to be sure that the mayor was in bed.

Kennedy knew where Kelly usually slept in the cabin. He blazed away, aiming about four shots at that bed. Then he wheeled his horse and raced away before the town woke up.

His shots were well aimed. One bullet went through the door, passed through some quilts and a plaster partition and struck Fannie Keenan in the side, killing her instantly.

Apparently gloating over having killed the mayor, Kennedy went to the one saloon still open. But when Wyatt Earp and Bat Masterson, both law officers, came in, Kennedy escaped, riding east.

The officers arrested a man they had seen with Kennedy. The man said he knew nothing about the shooting other than that he had heard the shots. He admitted he thought James Kennedy had fired the shots but he didn't know what he had shot at.

Before long, the news was all over town that Dora Hand had been shot. The coroner held an inquest. The verdict was that Dora Hand (Fannie Keenan) had met her death from a bullet fired presumably by James Kennedy.

Wyatt Earp was the city marshal and Bat Masterson was deputy U. S. marshal. They knew Kennedy and reasoned that, although he had raced off to the east, he would circle back and cross the Cimmaron River on his way south.

They rode through a stormy night, arriving at the river ford at sun-up. There was no sign anyone had crossed the ford recently so they waited, realizing that they might have guessed wrong.

About four in the afternoon, they saw Kennedy coming cautiously toward the ford. The officers waited to spring the trap. When they did, Kennedy wheeled to make a getaway instead of surrendering.

Bat Masterson swung up his rifle and fired, hitting Kennedy in the arm. But still he raced on. Wyatt Earp wanted to bring him in alive so he shot his horse. When the horse fell, Kennedy was pinned under him.

The officers pulled him from under the horse. When Kennedy heard he had killed Dora Hand instead of Mayor Kelly, he swore at Bat for not killing him when he had the chance.

Taking Kennedy to Dodge City, the lawmen got three doctors to tend to his arm.

Interior of the Long Branch Saloon, Dodge City, Kansas

Kansas State Historical Society

Several inches of the bone had to be removed. He would never use his right arm again.

He was in bad shape for some time but was finally brought to trial. Kennedy's wealthy father came to Dodge City and hired the best lawyers available. Kennedy finally got off because they couldn't prove that he had fired the shot that killed Dora Hand.

Kennedy recovered enough to get into another gun fight, using his left hand. He was good enough to win. But then he met a man who was better, and his career as a gunfighter abruptly ended.

Mysterious Murder
Barber County — March, 1879

It took three men to pull off the murder, if, indeed, it was a murder. Maybe it was just a convenient accident. Or maybe it happened just as the survivor said.

A man named Levy Baldwin owned a large farm in Douglas County. He hired two men, Brown and Hillman, to work the farm.

Baldwin was interested in some farm land in southwestern Kansas in Barber County. Why he sent his hired hands to look at the land instead of going himself is just another bit of the mystery surrounding the incident.

A short time before he sent his men to look at the land, Baldwin hired another man named Walters. He sent him along with Hillman and Brown on the trip to Barber County.

The trio arrived without mishap. But then one morning, Brown went into Medicine Lodge to report an accident had occurred at his camp the previous night. Brown said he had reached into the wagon for his bedroll and somehow his rifle got tangled up in the bedding and accidentally discharged. The bullet hit Hillman in the back of the head. And he fell forward into the fire. His face was terribly disfigured by the time Brown got the body out of the fire.

The story sounded honest to the officials who investigated the accident. But the questions began to bubble up when Mrs. Hillman tried to collect on the many life insurance policies that her husband had taken out. The insurance companies felt it was highly unusual for a man who earned thirty dollars a month to take out insurance policies that totaled $25,000. The companies demanded proof that the dead man was Hillman.

When the death was first recorded, the coroner had found no sign of foul play. They had to exhume the body. But the face of the dead man was so terribly disfigured by the fire that identification was impossible.

Hillman was gone, either dead or doing a perfect disappearing act. So was the new hired man, Walters. But not many people knew he even existed. Levy Baldwin said nothing about him. Neither did Brown. Hillman and Brown were strangers in the country. The situation showed one man dead and his partner reporting how he died, nothing more. It was assumed that everything had happened just as reported.

Hillman's life insurance policies had been written by several companies, none of which held a really large policy. But the companies got together and reached the conclusion that something was unnatural about the whole situation. No thirty dollar-a-month farmworker insured his life for $25,000. He couldn't afford it. Levy Baldwin, Hillman's employer, had underwritten Hillman's notes for the initial payments. But no payments had been made. So Hillman's beneficiary, his widow, stood to gain $25,000 dollars without anyone paying a cent in premiums.

The case dragged on in court for many years with no way to prove that the dead man was or was not Hillman. For the very few who knew that Baldwin had hired Walters and had sent him with Hillman and Brown to check out the land, it must have seemed strange that Walters disappeared the very night that Hillman was accidentally shot.

After many years, the insurance commissioner of Kansas ordered the insurance companies to pay up or get out of the state.

A compromise was struck and the case was closed.

Six months later, a paper was found that alleged the Hillmans, Brown and their employer, Baldwin, had schemed to defraud the insurance companies. The four were to share the profits. It had been the new man, Walters, who had been shot and pushed into the fire. The paper's authenticity was questioned. Some thought one of the insurance companies had left it where it would be found.

But the paper was dismissed and the mystery survived. A few people had seen Hillman when he first arrived in Barber County and they were convinced that the body was his. Hillman was never seen again.

Some people thought that justice had not been done. Some were sure that Baldwin and Brown, believing Hillman would show up to collect his share of the money, had killed him to make sure their own part in the plot wasn't exposed. But what had happened to Walters if Hillman was the one who had been shot and fell into the fire?

The only thing that is certain is that one man was dead and another had disappeared. The rest of the story always will be open to speculation.

Cock-eyed Frank Kills Levi
Ford County — April 5, 1879

The fight involving Cock-eyed Frank Loving and Levi Richardson, was apparently the climax of a long running argument. Some said the core of the argument was a woman both men wanted. Richardson was twenty-eight years old and Loving about twenty-five.

Levi Richardson was a freighter and Frank Loving was a gambler. There didn't seem to be any reference to gambling in the story of their argument. The possibility of a woman being involved was undeniable. The two had argued several times before and everyone knew there was bad blood between them.

The editor of the *Ford County Globe* didn't mince words. He wrote that the confrontation could easily have been avoided. But both men were confident of their abilities. "They fought because they wanted to fight."

According to witnesses, Richardson was just leaving the Long Branch Saloon when he met Loving coming in. Richardson turned right around and came back through the batwings. Loving sat down on a table and Richardson sat down not far from him. Apparently, neither man said anything for a while. Then Loving told Richardson if he had anything to say, say it to his face. Richardson snapped back that he didn't think Loving would fight, anyway. Loving said, "Try me and see."

Some witnesses said Richardson pulled his gun first; others said Loving did. Considering the fact that Richardson was a freighter and Loving a gambler, both were surely very familiar with guns.

Spectators agreed that Loving's first shot was a misfire. Ammunition wasn't always reliable. It wasn't unusual for ten percent of commercial shells to misfire. Loving obviously had a dud cartridge under the hammer of his gun. Richardson was either too excited or too furious to control himself. His bullets came close to Loving but only one even scratched him.

Loving's gun fired the second time he pulled the trigger and this time the bullet hit Richardson in the chest. One witness said it set his clothes on fire. Richardson kept firing but he had little control over his gun. Loving fired until his gun was empty. Richardson was hit again but he struggled to stay on his feet and keep fighting. He finally fell close to the stove they had been dodging around. Loving leaned over and snapped his gun twice more. But he was already out of bullets.

Loving was held until a coroner's jury had examined Richardson and reviewed the witnesses' statements. The jury's verdict was that Levi Richardson had come to his death from a bullet fired by Frank Loving in self-defense.

Kipple Murder
Ellis County — May, 1879

Four miles east of Hays, Kansas was the little settlement of Toulon. In the late 1870s, homesteaders had settled most of the land in the area. William Stackhouse settled on the east half of Section Eight. He had a wife and five sons. William's brother, Charles, who was deaf, lived with them.

The northwest quarter of Section Eight was claimed by Samuel Kipple. The Kipples had two sons who were fifteen and twenty years old. The southwest quarter of Section Eight was claimed by Cornelius Smith. Southwest of Smith, on the corner of Section Eighteen, was the land claimed by Isaac Wilcox and his son, Levi.

It was a typical homestead neighborhood except that the Stackhouses and the Kipples did not get along. It was obvious that each family wished that the other one would move away.

It was the desire to get rid of his neighbor that prompted William Stackhouse to coax his young neighbor, Levi Wilcox, to jump Kipple's claim before he had time to prove up on it. Levi Wilcox apparently liked the idea of having his own place instead of living with his father.

So Levi quickly built a small sod house on a corner of Kipple's land. He immediately moved into his new house with his young wife and tiny baby.

At first, Kipple couldn't believe that anyone would actually try to live on the land he owned so he didn't attempt to dislodge Wilcox. Then he realized that Levi really was building a house and he took action. There was no way two families could share one quarter of land.

He made his first move on May 25, 1879, when Levi Wilcox went to town and his wife, after putting the baby to sleep, walked the short distance to the Cornelius Smith dugout, on the southwest quarter of Section Eight, for a brief visit.

It was while she was there that Samuel Kipple and his two sons decided to visit the Wilcoxes. They were surprised when they found no one at home. They took advantage of the opportunity. They quickly tore down the walls of the soddy, never realizing there was a baby inside the house. With the walls crumbling, the dirt roof caved in. It covered the Wilcox baby.

The baby's mother saw what had happened and she raced up the steps of the Smith dugout and fairly flew across to her home. She rescued the baby unharmed. But the first blow had been struck.

Levi Wilcox, supported by William Stackhouse, decided to rebuild his soddy. They selected a site halfway between the ruined soddy and Smith's dugout but still on Kipple land. Within half a day, they had built up the walls to nearly three feet high.

About two o'clock, the two Kipple boys sneaked down to a buffalo wallow within thirty yards of the new construction and fired several revolver shots at the workers.

Photo courtesy Bob Chew, great-grandson of Lew Chew

Atchinson Police Officer Lew Chew

No one was injured but tempers were raging.

Samuel Kipple was in town talking to a lawyer about getting Wilcox off his land. William Stackhouse headed for Hays to get a warrant sworn out for the arrest of the two Kipple boys for the shooting incident.

That evening, the men at Smith's saw a figure near the new soddy. William Stackhouse also saw the man. He grabbed his rifle and hurried over to Smith's. He brought along his deaf brother, Charles. Cornelius Smith brought out his big rifle and handed it to Charles Stackhouse. The Stackhouse brothers, armed with rifles, and Levi Wilcox and another neighbor, Chester Rauch, carrying revolvers, started across some plowed ground toward the new Wilcox house.

The men got close enough to see Samuel Kipple standing at the corner of the new soddy, leaning on his broom-handle cane and looking at the sod walls.

Two shots roared almost as one and Kipple toppled forward. The four men turned and ran without waiting to see what damage they had done.

The next morning, the constable, coming out from Hays with warrants for the arrest of the two Kipple boys, found Samuel Kipple's body and went back to report to the sheriff.

The sheriff and the coroner came back. A coroner's jury was impaneled and came along. The jury reached the decision that Kipple had died from a bullet probably fired by William Stackhouse. Kipple had been killed on his own land. Sheriff Howard immediately arrested William Stackhouse.

Examining the plowed field and the soddy where Kipple was killed, they saw where the four armed men had stood and also where the bullet that had killed Kipple had gone through a pine board and then into Kipple's head.

William Stackhouse insisted that the fatal shot had been fired by his brother, Charles, who was deaf and didn't understand that they were only trying to scare Kipple. The sheriff employed a gun expert who set up the pine board and fired both rifles at it. Charles' gun didn't penetrate the board; William's did. William was charged with the murder.

Charles disappeared. William was tried and convicted and sentenced to twelve years in prison. When Charles was found, he was tried and found not guilty. Then with Charles legally exonerated, the prosecuting attorney asked Charles if he had killed Kipple. Charles said he had. The attorney thought he had sent the wrong man to prison and worked for years to get William pardoned. He finally succeeded after William had served nine of his twelve years.

Then a letter was found that proved that Charles, terribly excited by all the action

that he couldn't hear, had fired his rifle into the air. William Stackhouse was indeed the killer. The prosecuting attorney had not sent the wrong man to prison.

Shootout at Atchison
October 26, 1879

Atchison, Kansas was a wild town in 1859 when it was the starting point for the Leavenworth Cutoff and Pike's Peak Express Company Road to the new town of Denver. Goods from the north came down the Missouri River from shipping points in Iowa and were unloaded at Atchison and sent out on the L & PP freight and stage line.

Twenty years later, Atchison was considered a quiet, civilized town. It had a fine police force and, according to the Atchison Globe, one of the finest of the policemen was Lew Chew.

Lew Chew was a big man with a big reputation and a flawless record. Few citizens questioned his courage or his determination to uphold the law. But that didn't include those who allowed their reasoning to be clouded by whiskey.

Chew's challenge came suddenly from an unexpected source on a peaceful Sunday morning.

Amos Monroe was a quiet, peaceable black man when he was sober. But he loved his liquor. He had a reputation as a dangerous man when intoxicated.

According to witnesses, Monroe had disrupted the peace in Crall's Saloon, on Saturday night, after tipping the bottle a few too many times. Someone had restored peace by knocking Monroe down with a chair.

Apparently Monroe had not sobered up the next morning when he went into John Kafler's billiard hall. The bartender, Peter Anderson, was standing on the bar, cleaning the mirror. All the bottles had been moved to the bar beside him while he worked.

Monroe demanded a drink and told Anderson to put it on the account of another man. Anderson refused. Monroe proceeded to help himself from the bottles.

Anderson jumped down from the bar and grabbed a mallet to drive Monroe out of the hall. Monroe dodged away and whipped out a revolver and poked it in the bartender's face, demanding that he be given a drink.

Peter Anderson was no coward. He continued to refuse to give Monroe a drink, citing the law that said liquor couldn't be sold on Sunday. In spite of the fact that Monroe had a gun, he didn't use it or even renew his threat. Whirling, Monroe left the billiard hall.

Lew Chew was making his rounds and stopped at the billiard hall. After hearing Anderson's report, he knew he had to disarm Monroe before his whiskey-fogged temper caused serious trouble.

He found Monroe not far away. He called for him to stop; he wanted to talk to him. Monroe ignored him and Chew repeated his call.

Monroe wheeled, gun in hand, and fired. The bullet hit Chew in the left groin and knocked him to the sidewalk. But Chew was not out of the battle. He managed to draw his gun and fired at Monroe. His bullet went true, slamming into his opponent's breast.

Monroe was down now, too, but he managed to fire again. His coordination, however, was gone and the bullet missed. Chew did not have to fire again.

Monroe was carried into J. W. Allen's drug store where he died in a few minutes. The funeral was that afternoon.

Lew Chew was cared for but internal bleeding could not be stopped and he died that afternoon. He was only thirty-four years old and he left a wife and five children. He also left a reputation of being one of the fairest, most courageous policemen in Atchison.

IV
1880 — 1889

Last of the Trail Drives

Battle Across the Tracks
Ford County — April 16, 1881

Dodge City was changing. Before the first Texas herd arrived in 1881, the mayor posted a sign at the edge of town that no newcomer could fail to notice.

"All thieves, thugs, confidence men, and persons without visible means of support will take notice that the ordinance passed for their special benefit will be vigorously enforced after April 7, 1881."

The town was reaching for respectability and, at the same time, trying not to offend the cowboys. In spite of their rowdiness, the cowboys had plenty of 'means of support' when they got paid for their work on the trail. After that was gone, the new decree might very well bare its teeth at them. The cowboys might be powder kegs that exploded but it was usually the men who ignored the laws who served as the lighted fuses.

It seemed there was always a Masterson involved in life in Dodge City. Bat Masterson followed his friend, Wyatt Earp, when Earp left Dodge City for Tombstone, Arizona. Then Bat showed up on the gambler trail in New Mexico. Ed Masterson was killed on the streets of Dodge City. The younger brother, James, the city marshal of Dodge City, had

Kansas State Historical Society
James Masterson

apparently settled down in a business with a partner, A. J. Peacock, running a dance hall and gambling parlor.

The first sign that James Masterson might also get into trouble came when he voiced his criticism of their bartender, Al Updegraff. Updegraff was Peacock's brother-in-law. James Masterson was not satisfied with the bartender's work and told his partner that he should fire him. Peacock refused.

The argument quickly evolved into a feud with hot words and insults flying back and forth. Suspecting that it might end in a shooting war, James sent word to his brother, Bat, in New Mexico. Bat dropped everything and headed for Dodge City. He had lost one brother in Dodge. He didn't intend to lose another.

Bat suspected that Marshal James Masterson's enemies would be waiting for him. They would know that James had sent for Bat. So Bat jumped off the train before it stopped.

As Bat moved toward the depot, the train rolled on into the station, revealing the bartender, Updegraff, and his brother-in-law, A. J. Peacock, on the other side of the track, obviously watching for Bat to get off the train.

Bat called to them, saying he wanted to talk. The two recognized Bat's voice even before they saw him. Instead of stopping to talk, they dived behind the jail which was close to the tracks on the south side.

The older Masterson was caught out in the open but the railroad grade was about three feet high. He dashed up close to the grade and flattened himself on the ground, lifting his head just enough to see over the rails.

Updegraff and Peacock fired at Masterson but they had little chance of hitting him behind the railroad grade. Bat fired at the jail, knocking splinters from the corner where the two were hiding.

It could easily have been a stand-off if the citizens of Dodge City hadn't taken sides in the argument long before Bat arrived. Now they grabbed guns and did more than just talk about their preferences. A Masterson ally probably fired the rifle slug that hit Updegraff. There were many people who bought into the fight until, for three or four minutes, it resembled an all-out war.

Bullets smashed into the stores behind Bat. Some liquor stores, a drug store – even the Long Branch Saloon – got hit by bullets that apparently were intended for Masterson.

When the fighting was over, Updegraff was taken to a doctor. They didn't think he would live, but he did. A deputy marshal arrested Masterson.

Bat was charged with "discharging a pistol on the streets of the city." He paid the eight dollar fine and left town. James Masterson resigned as city marshal and left Dodge City with his brother.

Dodge City citizens thought they had eliminated the gunfighters when the Mastersons left town. They were wrong.

The Killing of Mike Meagher
Sumner County —
December, 1881

The trouble started in Wichita in 1876. Mike Meagher was town marshal. In handling a tough situation one day, he killed an outlaw named Powell. The papers barely mentioned his death. However, Powell had a cousin, Jim Talbott, who did take note of his passing and vowed vengeance. He was just waiting for the right opportunity.

Talbott's chance came five years later in Caldwell, Kansas, near the Oklahoma border. Caldwell had a reputation as a wild town. Mike Meagher was mayor. Jim Talbott rounded up eight tough gun hands and rode into Caldwell.

Talbott guessed correctly that a gang of that size would startle the lawmen of the town into calling in reserves. And he was sure that one of those reserves would be the mayor. In the fight, Talbott intended to kill Meagher. He even bragged about his mission in a local saloon.

A man named George Speer owned that saloon and he had a bone to pick with Meagher, too. Meagher had once arrested Speer's brother. So he joined with Talbott's crew. They expected to overpower the lawmen with sheer numbers.

Talbott called on his men to start a ruckus that would bring out the law. It worked and the marshal, as Talbott expected, called for help, especially Mike Meagher, the ex-marshal.

Many of the citizens of the town joined in and it became a free-for-all. Wagons and storefronts were peppered with bullets. It was a wild melee. Meagher lost track of who he was fighting and didn't see Talbott swing around one of the stores. Talbott came up behind Meagher and shot him in the back.

Talbott knew Meagher had a fatal wound. He called for his men and they raced for their horses and thundered out of town. Only one of the fleeing gunmen was killed and that was the saloon owner, George Speer.

It was years before Talbott was located and brought in to stand trial. By then, most of the witnesses of the fight were either dead or had moved away. Jim Talbott was never convicted of the murder of one of Kansas's fine lawmen.

Burning the Evidence
Cowley County — October 2, 1882

To a cowboy or a man who depends on a horse for his livelihood or, in many cases, for his life itself, there is no punishment too severe for a horse thief or,

even worse, a man who deliberately kills a horse.

Down in Winfield, Kansas, the shriek of "Fire!" exploded over the town at four o'clock in the morning and everyone's peaceful sleep was shattered.

Clothes were thrown on and every man and most of the women raced out to see the fire. No one had to ask directions. Flames roared into the sky and tinted the dark cloud of smoke a terrifying red.

The livery barn was burning. There was a tank of water outside the barn but the heat was too fierce for anyone to get close to the tank. There was a pump farther away but the tiny stream of water it produced would fill no more that two buckets a minute. They needed hundreds of gallons of water every minute to stop the blaze.

All volunteer firefighters could do was stand back and watch the barn go up in smoke. The screams of the horses tied in their stalls finally ceased. It was Sunday morning but few were in the mood to go to church.

It was Monday morning before the ashes cooled enough to assess the damage and try to find the cause of the fire. The losses were staggering. The barn was the biggest livery barn in Winfield.

Some men checked the material losses while others tried to identify the carcasses of the horses. The total was horrendous. Consumed by the fire were four busses and a large number of carriages, a bin full of grain and loft full of hay. But the loss that hit most of them the hardest was the total of twenty-six horses burned to death.

A check of the horses that had been stalled in the barn that night was twenty-eight. Two were not in the ashes.

It didn't take long for some men to jump to a very logical conclusion. Someone had stolen two horses then set the barn on fire to cover up his tracks.

Valley Falls, Kansas, 1879, from the top of the Octagon Hotel.

Kansas State Historical Society

Some watchers doubted the theory. No man could be so vile and cruel as to burn over twenty horses alive! But there were twenty-six carcasses in the ashes. They tried to identify the dead horses but with little success.

A lawyer in town, A. B. Taylor, kept a very valuable trotting horse in the stable and he was certain that his horse was one of the two that were missing. Some ridiculed the idea. The lawyer was convinced that the fire had been set to cover up a theft. And what horse was more likely to be stolen than his fancy trotting horse?

Sheriff Cope went along with that idea and began searching the country for the trotting horse. If he found that horse, he was sure he'd have the man who burned the twenty-six horses. Either the theft or the burning was a crime certainly worthy of a hanging.

It took a few days but the sheriff found the trotting horse in Derby, a town in Sedgwick County, just south of Wichita. Sheriff Cope sent a telegram to A. B. Taylor to come and identify the horse. Taylor went there and claimed his animal.

The thief apparently had run out of money and sold the horse for ten dollars. The man who had bought the horse described the fugitive in detail. Sheriff Cope was positive he could catch him and he vowed to do it no matter how long it took.

If he did catch the thief, the sheriff knew he couldn't take his prisoner back to Winfield. He'd be lynched on sight in spite of the law's protection. But what difference did it make whether it was legal or not? The man who had stolen two horses and burned twenty-six others alive deserved nothing better than a six-foot rope and a ten-foot drop.

A Senseless Murder
Jefferson County —
January 6, 1883

Ever since the days when men began carrying guns, the cry for gun control has been heard. It has not changed.

The newspapers of more than a century ago were calling for control of guns, especially among the young.

Those who advocated no one but police be allowed to carry guns were given ammunition for their arguments by an incident that occurred in the peaceful community of Valley Falls, Kansas in early 1883.

Charles Cobb had always been fascinated with guns and carried a firearm as soon as he was old enough to sneak one out of the house. On the evening of January 5, Charles Cobb attended a debate at a local school house. He got into an argument with another youth, Henry McClenny. After the meeting ended, Cobb renewed the argument with McClenny and, before it was over, Cobb drew his gun and fired it several times. Apparently, he didn't intend to kill anyone. But his thoughtfulness was not appreciated by McClenny. McClenny went to town the next morning, Saturday, January 6, and swore out a warrant for Cobb's arrest for disturbing the peace.

The warrant was given to Constable Daniel Weiser. Weiser couldn't find any officer to go with him to make the arrest so he took his son, Robert. They went to the home of Louis Cobb, the father of Charles.

Mr. and Mrs. Cobb were highly respected people in Valley Falls. All their children except Charles were well behaved.

Charles had grown up quarreling with anyone who disagreed with him. In his teens, he mingled with those who lived by their guns. It was generally believed that he placed no value on any human life except his own.

Daniel and Robert Weiser arrived at the Cobb place about noon. They hadn't been told that Charles Cobb had been in town during the forenoon and bought a big pocketful of cartridges for his Winchester rifle. He also had a few drinks and bragged that nobody was going to arrest him. He obvious-

ly had heard that McClenny had sworn out the arrest warrant.

Leaving the buggy in the yard, the two Weisers went to the two-room house occupied by the Cobb family. Robert went to the north door while his father waited south of the house. Robert went into the house and found himself facing Charles Cobb, who pointed a rifle at him.

Louis Cobb and his family were trying to get Charles to put down the rifle. But the wild young man apparently felt he was above any correction or restraints of his family. Louis Cobb shut the partition door between Charles and Robert Weiser.

Charles backed out the other door and into the yard, still holding the rifle to his shoulder. His family surrounded him, trying to convince him to put down the weapon. He paid no attention.

Daniel Weiser called for Charles to drop the rifle and come into town with him. Charles ignored that, too. Weiser drew his gun and fired a warning shot. It missed Charles but nicked one of the Cobb children.

Charles dodged around the corner of the house and Robert started after him. When he got on that side of the house, he discovered that Charles was not in sight.

Suddenly Charles rose up from behind the well curbing. He shot once, hitting Robert in the arm. Robert was out of the fight and he began running toward the buggy. There was a fence between him and the buggy. Daniel Weiser went after his son.

Charles fired again, this time at Daniel. His shot hit Weiser in the back, the bullet going all the way through him. Daniel said clearly, "I am killed," but then climbed the fence and made his way to a stone where he sat down and died.

There could have been no better argument for taking guns away from children and young people who haven't reached a

Wright Beverly & Co. The Long Branch is under the awning.

Kansas State Historical Society

level of maturity where they can control themselves.

The newspapers for some time were filled with articles and editorials about the need for a law to take the guns away from irresponsible people like Charles Cobb. But there was no mention of the murderer's fate.

The Death of an Innocent
Ford County — July 1883

Dodge City usually was hot in July. But the nights were often just cool enough to bring out the playfulness in grown men. Three such men rode into Dodge that July night and two of them spent too much time in the saloons. Their friend, Johnny Ballard, stayed sober.

Johnny probably had a reason for not drinking. He knew his comrades' penchant for making amusements where none were intended. As the evening wore on, he saw it was going to be one of those times.

After he felt they'd had enough fun and it was already past time to get back to camp, Johnny managed to get his friends out of the last saloon they tried to drink dry. But get-

ting them on their horses and out of town was a bigger chore.

He herded the two toward the bridge and the trail to their camp. But just before they reached the bridge, they passed Bond and Nixon's Dance Hall. Jerking their horses toward the hitch rack, the pair slid out of their saddles and wobbled toward the door.

All Johnny could do was wait. This time it wasn't a long delay. But when they stumbled out to their horses, they still were looking for more excitement. Johnny was interested only in getting them across the bridge and headed for camp.

Still a short distance from the bridge, one of the men jerked out his gun and fired it in the air. His partner joined him and they began shooting up the town. Nobody could explain why drunken cowboys got so much joy out of shooting up store fronts.

The law officers of Dodge saw none of the fun and they joined in the shooting. But their targets were not the store fronts. They were aiming at the cowboys who were disturbing a peaceful evening.

Johnny knew they had to ride for it. He was in the lead and he was sure his partners would be right behind him. There was noth-

Courtesy John W. Nixon, Vice President, First National Bank, Medicine Lodge

The First National Bank of Medicine Lodge, as it looked at the time of the 1884 robbery.

ing like bullets snapping past his ears to sober up a drunken cowboy.

The officers scored their first and only hit just as the men reached the bridge. It was hard to explain how Johnny Ballard, well out in front of the others, was the one who caught the bullet.

Johnny, shot through the head, slid off his horse at the foot of the bridge, dead before he hit the ground. Nobody took credit for that shot. Johnny was well liked by all and never caused any trouble.

The *Ford County Globe* summed up the feeling of Dodge City. "It was a very unfortunate affair that young Ballard should pay the penalty for others' crimes."

Lynchings at Medicine Lodge Barber County — May 1, 1884

The country was becoming more civilized than it was in the days when people settled problems permanently

John W. Nixon Photo

E. W. Payne bank president in 1884

The posse that captured the Medicine Lodge bank robbers.

Courtesy John W. Nixon, Vice President, First National Bank, Medicine Lodge

on the spot, often with a short rope and a long drop. But Medicine Lodge, Kansas was a contradiction. Some things simply could not wait for the law to grind out a punishment that often did not fit the crime. So far as the citizens of Medicine Lodge were concerned, there was only one punishment that could do justice to the crime that was committed against their community.

Shortly after nine o'clock on the morning of May 1, 1884, the "sons of Beelzebub" exploded the peace of Medicine Lodge. It was raining heavily and trouble other than the weather was the farthest thing from the minds of the people in town.

Businesses were open but they weren't expecting much traffic because of the weather. But one place had some customers within minutes after its door opened.

No one noticed the four riders who came in from the west and tied their horses behind the coal shed at the rear of the bank.

Only a few people saw them come around to the front door and three of them go into the bank. In their rain gear, they were indistinguishable from other wet customers who wanted to get their business done and get home out of the rain.

Although the visitors were in a hurry, their business was not routine. Inside the bank, the three men split up. One went to the window of the cashier, George Geppert, another to the window of the president of the bank, E. W. Payne. and the third went into the back room The fourth man stood guard in front of the bank.

Exactly what happened next had to be pieced together after some of the town's citizens got into the bank. The four visitors had come to town to rob the bank and they lost no time in getting to work. They hadn't been in the bank more than a minute when several shots rang out, alerting the people of town that there was mischief.

The captured bank robbers were photographed before they died. They are, from left: John Wesley, Henry Brown, Billie Smith and Ben Wheeler.

Courtesy John W. Nixon, Vice President, First National Bank, Medicine Lodge

Several people heard the shots and some close by sounded the alarm. Marshal Denn was standing near the livery stable directly across from the bank. He opened fire on the guard in front of the building. The guard fired back. Both men missed their targets but the war was on.

Inside the bank, the robbers panicked, realizing they had lost the element of surprise. They dashed out of the bank empty handed, charged around the corner to their horses and whipped them into a frantic run out of town.

Some men in town ran for their horses while others rushed to the bank to see what had happened. The robbers had been in the bank scarcely a minute. That wasn't nearly long enough to rob a bank. But it was long enough to do some terrible damage.

The robbers had shot George Geppert, the cashier, and he was dying. They also shot E. W. Payne. He was badly wounded. The robbers hadn't been in the bank long enough to be threatened or provoked into shooting. It was deliberate murder.

Both Geppert and Payne were prominent members of the community, honest and well liked. The fury of the town exploded.

It took only a very short time for men to get their horses and thunder off in pursuit of the robbers. Most of the posse members had no desire to capture the robbers. They wanted to give them what they had given the two officers in the bank – no chance. They had no intentions of bringing the fugitives back alive.

By the time the impromptu posse left town, the doctor had examined the two men shot in the bank. George Geppert was dead; E. W. Payne had a very serious wound from a bullet that had entered near the right shoulder and lodged under the left shoulder blade. He might survive.

The men in the posse pursuing the bank robbers were becoming aware that the outlaws were obviously not professionals. Professionals would not have resorted to murder before they got the money. And they didn't have the swiftest of horses for their escape.

The pursuers came in sight of the outlaws as they were crossing Medicine Lodge

The site of the hangings of the Medicine Lodge bank robbers now is a peaceful residential area.

Author's photo

Creek south of town, and they urged their horses to greater speed.

The outlaws began shooting at the posse even before they were close enough to be accurate with their shots. The posse returned the fire with no better luck.

Three posse members, led by a man named Charley Taliaferro, swung away from the others and raced around the outlaws until they had them in a crossfire. The robbers wheeled to the west, the only avenue left open to them, and spurred their weary horses toward the breaks in the gypsum hills.

But their effort to escape were matched and exceeded by the posse's determination to catch them. The fighting got hot when latecomers from town arrived.

Seeing they had no chance to escape, the robbers threw their guns down and their hands up. The fury of the posse had eased a bit and they accepted the surrender. Maybe it was because they saw no opportunity close at hand to hang the outlaws and that

made them willing to take them back to town. The determination to see that they paid for murdering one of the town's favorite people, George Geppert, had not faded.

The posse members got a shock when they got their first close look at the outlaws. They knew every one of them. The leader, in particular, startled them. Henry Brown was the marshal of Caldwell, Kansas, a town about sixty miles southeast of Medicine Lodge, near the Kansas-Oklahoma border. Another member of the gang was Ben Wheeler, assistant marshal of Caldwell. The other two were cowboys that most of the posse knew. One was William Smith of the T5 ranch. The other cowboy was less familiar, known simply as Wesley.

It was hard for the men of the posse to believe that the lawmen of a neighboring town would turn outlaw and actually shoot down an unarmed man. It was cold blooded murder.

According to rumors, Marshal Brown had once been a friend of Billy the Kid. As marshal of Caldwell, he had killed several men in the past three years. But in each case, it was declared to be in the line of duty.

Ben Wheeler, Brown's assistant, had no known criminal record. Yet it was Wheeler's bullet that had killed George Geppert. That branded Wheeler as perhaps the most cold blooded killer in the gang. Smith and Wesley, the two cowboys, had no record of being hardened criminals.

If the gang had successfully pulled off the robbery and killed both Geppert and Payne so there would have been no witnesses to identify them, they might have gone back to their jobs and no one would have suspected them of the crime.

The posse took the four prisoners back to Medicine Lodge. Their appearance was met by a chorus of "Hang them! Hang them!" The townspeople were stunned when they recognized the men. But it didn't replace the demand to make them pay for killing Geppert.

Marshal Denn, with the men he had deputized, had his hands full keeping citizens from tearing the prisoners away from him and hanging them immediately. But the marshal was in command and, as a lawman, he had to defend the prisoners. He got them into the jail and placed them under guard.

The people seethed around the jail but the calmer minds prevailed and the budding mob slowly dissolved. Its mood, however, did not soften. The town sank into ominous silence. The fact that the bank robbers hadn't stolen any money didn't matter. The murderers had killed one man and seriously wounded another. For that, they would pay.

The day faded away. It had been a day Medicine Lodge would never forget. Nor would residents forget how it ended.

At approximately nine o'clock, three pistol shots reverberated through the town and men appeared as if by magic from buildings on the street leading to the jail. The march was slow but determined. The marshal and his deputies made an effort to stop the mob but it was useless. They were overpowered and the men pushed into the jail.

The cell door was unlocked and men found the keys and unshackled the prisoners. The prisoners made a sudden dash through the jail door in a desperate attempt to escape the fate they knew was waiting for them.

But the mob was organized and prepared. A shotgun blast brought down the leader, Marshal Brown. Pistols roared and in the hail of lead, Wheeler was seriously wounded. The two cowboys threw up their hands and stopped.

One bank robber was dead and another wounded. But the vengeance-driven mob was not satisfied. They had come out to hang the killers.

The three live prisoners were herded down into the river bottom east of town where there were some big elm trees. The ropes were adjusted around the necks of the prisoners, the loose ends thrown over a massive limb.

The cowboys were silent. But Wheeler, the man who had killed Geppert, begged for mercy. Of all the ones captured, he was the least likely to receive sympathy.

Given an opportunity for any last words, Wesley asked that word of his death be sent to his friends in Vernon, Texas. Smith, also from Vernon, calmly requested that his saddle and possessions be sold and the money sent to his mother in Vernon.

In spite of their beliefs that lynching was wrong, the people of Medicine Lodge were convinced they had meted out the proper punishment for the killers.

Kansas State Historical Society
"Mysterious" Dave Mather

Tom Nixon Murder
Ford County — July 21, 1884

When gunmen stopped killing other gunmen, it should have marked the end of the wild days. But the wild days could hardly be considered gone when peace officers decided to kill other peace officers.

What better place for the killings to be prolonged than in Dodge City? The incident involved an assistant marshal and a deputy sheriff. The headline in the *Kansas Cowboy* on July 26, 1884, read: "Assistant Marshal Thomas Nixon Shot and Killed by Deputy Sheriff David Mather."

The trouble between the two apparently began several months earlier when the dance hall in the opera house, operated by Mather and Black, was closed. Mather blamed Nixon for the closing.

On the Friday night before the shooting, Nixon was looking through the window into the opera house where a performance was being presented. Mather, on the inside, saw him peeking through the window and rushed outside. But Nixon was leaving. Mather hurled a string of vile words after him. Nixon turned and fired his pistol in Mather's direction. The bullet cut a splinter from a board close to Mather. Nixon was arrested and tried in court on Monday but was acquitted.

Dave Mather had a gambler's face that never gave a hint of what he was thinking and he moved around as quietly as a cat. He had earned the nickname of 'Mysterious Dave.' Few people could call him a friend. Nobody spoke to him on the street because no one could be sure how he would respond. He had been over a large part of Kansas, often serving as a peace officer. He had served in Dodge City once before. There were stories afloat about the many men Mather had killed, most of them in the line of duty.

Tom Nixon, on the other hand, hadn't moved around much. He had been a buffalo hunter and had been in Dodge City when it was nothing more than just a place from which to ship hides. He had lived there longer than any other citizen. He was a man of the frontier – rough and sometimes crude, but honest in his dealings. All the early settlers called him a friend.

Mysterious Dave Mather apparently did not agree with the court that ruled Nixon had done no wrong in firing at Mather.

That July evening, Marshal Nixon came down to the opera house about ten o'clock and paused to observe the crowd coming and going. He was leaning against the wall supporting himself with his right hand.

Boot Hill Museum, Dodge City
Assistant Marshal Tom Nixon

Dave Mather came up the walk and, seeing Nixon, called to him. Nixon apparently didn't hear him and Mather called louder, "Tom!"

Nixon started to turn to see who had called him. It is doubtful if he ever saw who it was. As Nixon turned, Mather fired. He was only three or four yards away, according to witnesses who whirled around at the sound of the shot to see what was happening.

Those witnesses said that Nixon fell when the first bullet hit him. After he was on the ground, Mather fired three more times. There were four bullet wounds in Nixon's body when the coroner examined him. One bullet had pierced the heart and apparently was the first one to hit him. The last three were fired into the body at close range.

Sheriff Sughrue was summoned and he arrested Mather without incident. Mather went willingly to jail. Bond was set at $6,000. A group of leading merchants signed for the bond and Mather was released until the trial.

Every business place was closed for the funeral of Tom Nixon and many eulogies were delivered.

Mather's trial drew a large crowd. The eye witnesses gave their testimonies and the lawyers argued the points. The jury took only a short time to decide and they returned a verdict of not guilty.

There were many of Nixon's friends at the trial and they could not believe the jury could call it self defense when Nixon never touched his gun.

Baddest of the Bad
Ford County — September, 1885

The Tascosa stage was within a few miles of Dodge City when it happened. Three riders stopped the coach and yelled at the driver to open the mail sacks.

Grant Wells was inside the coach with a lady. His younger brother was riding a horse behind the coach. Two of the bandits began abusing the younger Wells boy, perhaps thinking that would convince the driver to obey their orders.

Grant Wells leaped out of the coach and demanded that they stop harrassing his brother, Wilford. The two bandits laughed at him and fired their guns at Wells. Neither scored a hit.

Wells returned the fire with one shot. That shot hit the leader in the forehead, killing him instantly. The other two bandits abandoned their fallen comrade and spurred their horses out of sight.

Prairie blizzards killed cattle, horses and people on the frontier and still are dangerous today.

Courtesy: Loral Johnson, Publisher, Imperial Republican.

Wells got back in the coach and it went on to Dodge City where he reported what had happened. Two men went out and brought in the body of the dead bandit. The hold-up hadn't looked like a professional job and what they found on the dead man proved that it wasn't.

Papers on the dead man identified him as Robert J. Robbins. Robbins and his two companions had arrived in Dodge City the previous week. Apparently, they were dead broke. There was a note in Robbins' pocket addressed to his mother:

"I am going to rob someone tonight ... I was raised by a good honest mother ... My father has gone before me and I will perhaps go tonight."

There was only a nickel in his pocket.

Grant Wells was a noted gunman, so killing Robbins was no great achievement. He was an assistant city marshal in Dodge. Ed Prather was a good friend of Wells and almost his equal with a gun.

One day City Marshal McCoy had a clash with Prather and his gang. In what was tagged as the "Green Front Fight." Prather was wounded in the leg. Before Prather could be arrested, Wells abandoned his assistant city marshal job and took his friend to a small ranch to recover from his wound far away from any lawman.

Prather recuperated and started a saloon business in partnership with Grant Wells. They thought highly of themselves and their skill with guns. As Prather put it, they were the "baddest of the bad." They put on a show to attract customers. Prather announced that he was the great grandson of William Tell. He put a tin can on his head and told Wells to shoot it off. Wells did.

Then Wells found a hard hat and perched it on his head and told Prather to shoot a hole through the hat. Prather complied. The show was going over with a flourish. Prather then bragged that he would put a bullet right through the hole he had previously made in Wells' hat. He wanted to prove he was as good a shot as Doc Carver, a marksman in Buffalo Bill's show.

A bit reluctantly, Wells put the hat back on his head. Prather jerked up his gun and fired, hitting Wells in the head, killing him.

The show ended right there. Prather left town hurriedly and eventually wound up in the county seat war at Leotia.

Some time later, Bill Tilghman, City Marshal of Leotia, killed Prather in self-defense.

The Worst Killer of All
Western Kansas — January 1886

New Year's Day in 1886 was a beautiful day and the citizens of Dodge City celebrated it with vigor. The town was settling down into a civilized city. The last of the cattle drives were history and the rowdy cowboys who shot up the town were gone. Dodge had a lot to look forward to in the new year.

Some of the young people were still making the rounds wishing everyone a happy new year, when a black cloud rolled in from the northwest. The wind hit with a blast that nearly knocked them off their feet. The snow was only a minute behind the wind.

Within two minutes, the snow was so thick people outside could scarcely breathe and they couldn't see more than a few feet. Being in town, they made their way back home, mostly from memory. The snow was wet and it stuck to clothes and soaked through to the skin.

The storm caused little damage to humans but it plastered livestock and chilled them to the bone. Most cattle survived this storm. But five days later, a storm struck that the cattle couldn't survive. This time the snow was not so wet but it came as a blinding blizzard and the temperature dropped to well below zero. It was a warning of what was to come. Southern Kansas seldom experienced such harsh weather.

The wind rose to more than forty miles an hour and the snow was so heavy a man could not see ten feet. Cattle turned their tails to the wind and drifted. Fences were smashed down and the cattle moved on. If the fences were strong, the cattle piled up against them and died there, trampled down by those following them.

That January proved to be one of the worst the residents of Kansas had ever seen.

Between January 12 and the 23, six more blizzards struck. Cattle losses ranged from twenty percent to one hundred percent. Many ranchers were put out of business.

When the snow finally melted, carcasses of cattle lined the fence rows. Many horses were also lost. Bodies of coyotes, antelope and deer dotted the prairie. The toll among the people was appalling. There were many belated funerals for people lost in the storms and not found until the melting snow revealed where they had died.

Cimarron-Ingalls
County Seat Fight
Gray County — January 2, 1889

In 1889, there was a bloody battle over the county seat in Gray County, which lies between Dodge City and Garden City. Cimarron was the county seat. But Ingalls, six miles west of Cimarron, challenged it for the title. Tempers rose and hot words were exchanged. An election was supposed to solve the dispute. But the results were challenged.

An Ingalls man, Newt Watson, was elected county clerk. Because he held the office, he demanded the county records be brought over from Cimarron to Ingalls. The people of Cimarron refused to relinquish the records. The county sheriff, Joe Reynolds, was at home nursing a gunshot wound he had received in the course of his duties.

The people of Ingalls resolved to get the records some way. Once they had the county files, they could claim the county seat because Cimarron couldn't conduct any county business.

To make sure they got the records, Ingalls residents brought out several well known gunmen from Dodge City, including Jim Masterson, Billy Tilghman, Ed Brooks, and several others. They would go with the

The citizens of Cimarron, left, and Ingalls, below, got into a shooting war in a dispute over which community would be the seat of government in Gray County. These photos were taken in the late 1800s.

Kansas State Historical Society photos

Author's photos

Cimarron and Ingalls as they look today

Ingalls men to take the records, with or without force.

The raiders, depending entirely on the size and quality of their armed squad, drove a wagon up to the courthouse door in Cimarron and began to bring out the records and load them in the wagon.

Four of the group, including Watson and Jim Masterson, were inside the building when the residents of Cimarron suddenly began to fire on them from every side. The men at the wagon were in real trouble. Tilghman was shot in the leg; Brooks was shot in the stomach; a man named Bolds was shot three times. Even the wagon driver, Charlie Reicheldeffer, was hit.

Everyone outside the courthouse managed to get into the wagon and Reicheldeffer slapped the team into a hard run, heading back to Ingalls.

The four men on the second floor of the courthouse fought back. The attackers got into the lower floor and shot up through the ceiling, hoping to hit some of the men above. But they climbed up on tables and cabinets and the steel safe.

The siege lasted for six hours. Then the town of Cimarron received a telegram from Bat Masterson saying that he would bring an army on the train if they didn't release the men in the courthouse immediately. Bat's brother was in the courthouse. The threat was understood. The siege was over. The casualty list revealed one dead and seven wounded.

There was a trial of the raiders for the death of a Cimarron man. They were acquitted. Cimarron is still the county seat today.

A sign outside the C. M. Condon Bank, describes
the to events of Oct. 5, 1892 when the Dalton
Gang rode into town.

Bob Dalton's name marks the spot in a
Coffeyville alley where the bank robber was
killed.

V
1890 — 1899

Day of the Gangs

C. M. Condon's bank, as it looks today. At right, Death Alley, where several Coffeyville residents, and Dalton Gang members died in the Oct. 5, 1892 shootout, after a foiled bank robbery.

The Dalton Gang
Montgomery County —
October 5, 1892

Many people remember a childrens' poem called *October's Bright Blue Weather*. It was just such a day on October 5, 1892, in Coffeyville, Kansas, in the southeast corner of Montgomery County, on the Oklahoma border.

But there was some planning going on that was not as bright as the October sunshine. Five men rode into Coffeyville and their thoughts were not on the sunny day. They wore fake sideburns or mustaches. They didn't want to be recognized. They were all well known in Coffeyville.

Few Coffeyville residents paid any attention to the strangers. Some did wonder about all the arms they were carrying – rifles and six-guns and plenty of ammunition.

It was a little past nine thirty and the town was going about its usual business. The stores were open and so were the banks. That was when the men came.

They rode along Eighth Street until they came to Maple Street where they reined to their right. At the alley they swung to the left and hitched their horses to the fence at the rear of Judge Munn's lot.

Then they began a march up the alley toward the plaza. Some people stared at them but nobody seemed to be alarmed by what they saw. Three of the men went through the door in the southwest corner of C. M. Condon's bank. The other two broke into a sprint across the plaza to the First National Bank and went in through the front door.

Within seconds the curtain rose on the drama that the five men had planned. But they hadn't anticipated the way it would end.

Guns appeared in the hands of the robbers and they demanded that all the money in the banks be put in sacks. Outside, a man who had seen the gunmen go into the banks realized what was going on and he yelled that the banks were being robbed. From that second on, the plan that the outlaws had woven so carefully began to unravel.

There was confusion outside the banks but the robbers tried to ignore that as they went about their business of cleaning out the cash. In the Condon Bank, one demanded the money in the safe but the cashier said the safe had a time lock on it and it couldn't be opened until the lock released.

The robber demanded to know when the vault would be opened. He was told that it unlocked at exactly 9:45. That was just three minutes away. The robber's inexperience revealed itself then. He said he'd wait. Three minutes was not long to wait to get all the money in the safe.

But before the three minutes were up, a rifle outside roared and the bullet slammed through the plate glass front of the bank.

Kansas State Historical Society

Tombstone marking the graves of three of the bank robbers.

Author's photo

The type of coffin used to bury the Daltons.

More guns joined in. All the bank workers flopped down flat on the floor.

The thieves realized that their plans were suddenly as worthless as a spent bullet. They began firing at the men in the plaza. It quickly became obvious that their only hope was to get away as fast as possible. All three dashed out the door.

Over in the First National Bank, the other two robbers had better success in collecting money. They stuffed several thousand dollars into a big sack. But the roar of gunfire stopped the collection.

One man, Emmett Dalton, the youngest of the Dalton brothers, clutched the sack full of money as he and his brother Bob prepared to make their escape. Pushing the teller, W. H. Sheppard, and the cashier, Thomas Ayers, ahead of them, they headed for the front door. But the moment they appeared there, someone took a shot at them.

Leaping back inside, they slammed the door shut. Wheeling toward the back door, they pushed the hostages ahead of them as shields and stepped out into the alley, turning north toward Eighth Street, trying to get around the plaza where most of the shooting seemed to be concentrated.

A young man, Lucius Baldwin, only twenty-three, was coming down from Eighth Street. He had a revolver in his hand but he apparently mistook the men with Sheppard and Ayers as men defending the bank. The robbers made no mistake about Baldwin. If he recognized them, he would shoot them. Bob Dalton would not trust his luck any farther. He threw up his Winchester rifle and fired, killing Baldwin. He was only the first of several who would die before the shooting stopped.

The robbers released their two hostages so they could move faster. Emmett took the lead, carrying the sack of money while Bob brought up the rear, his rifle ready to fire at any threat. As they crossed Union Street, they saw armed men down close to the front door of the First National Bank where the Daltons had entered only minutes before. Standing in the doorway of Ramel's Drug store was 36-year-old George Cubine with a rifle in his hand, looking at the front of the bank next door. Bob Dalton fired at him. the bullet hitting him in the back and going through his heart.

Running farther along the street, Dalton saw 60-year-old Charles Brown just a few feet from Cubine. He had grabbed Cubine's rifle and was looking for whoever had shot him. Bob Dalton shot Brown in the chest and he fell almost on top of Cubine. In less than a minute, Bob Dalton had killed three men, all held in high esteem by their neighbors.

Ayers, the cashier, had run to Isham's Hardware on the other side of the bank as soon as he was released. Now he stepped out with a rifle in his hand. Dalton fired at him. The bullet made a terrible wound in Ayer's face and neck but wasn't fatal.

Then Bob and Emmett Dalton passed behind Condon's Bank and were out of sight of the plaza. They turned south in the alley to the west of the Condon bank and joined the other robbers at the junction of the alley and the east-west alley they had used coming toward the plaza. They had only a few yards to go to reach their horses.

But the distance the robbers had to cover were the hardest yards they would ever travel. Many men in town now had grabbed guns and followed the three robbers from Condon's Bank into the alley.

The next three minutes were pandemonium. Only as the participants reviewed it later could details be sorted out. The citizens of Coffeeville were unarmed when the robbery began. But the hardware store was well stocked with guns and ammunition and it was those rifles and shotguns that cut down the Dalton gang. When the people realized that their neighbors were being killed, they rose in a frenzy to wipe out the killers.

The fighting was furious in the alley as the Daltons attempted to get to their horses. Bob Dalton was the first man to go down. He may have been pinpointed if the local fighters knew that he had killed three well respected men already. Even after he was hit, he fired more shots, spraying them at random. One lodged in a window sill only two inches from fifty pounds of dynamite.

That explosion would probably have brought the battle to a thunderous conclusion. But it was the end for Bob Dalton in any case.

Grat Dalton, the oldest of the three Daltons in this fight, was badly wounded but he managed to prop himself up enough to fire his gun. He shot Marshal Connelly in the back. Connelly was forty-seven years old and was the last of the natives to die in the fight.

Grat was still trying to get to the horses and he crawled painfully past the body of the marshal but, just beyond, John Kloehr, Connelly's companion, ended Grat Dalton's career with a rifle bullet.

Emmett Dalton, the youngest brother, was hit several times. But he did get to his horse and he still had the sack of money he had taken from the First National Bank. He managed to get into the saddle. But then he came back and reached a hand down to his brother, Bob, to help him up on the horse with him. That was the moment when a shotgun blast from a man named Seamen brought him down. He already had a broken arm and bullets in both hips.

The two robbers who were not Daltons had not fared well, either. One, William Powers (some knew him as Tom Evans), was dead. The other, Richard Broadwell, alias John Moore, alias Texas Jack, had managed to get away. As soon as the melee was over, several men took up Moore's trail. They found him just a half mile away where he had fallen from his horse and died from his wounds.

The scene in the narrow alley was one that those who saw it would never forget. In a space no more than thirty feet long and ten feet wide, four men lay dead and others, including Emmett Dalton, lay wounded. Blood was everywhere.

The sack of money in Emmett Dalton's possession contained more than $21,000. It was returned to the bank and that night when the banks balanced their books, they were only $20 short.

Emmett Dalton, in spite of his terrible wounds, did survive to spend some time in prison and ended his life as a law abiding citizen.

One Wild Cowboy's Career
Ford County — 1892

To itemize or even outline the career of one of the wild cowboys who populated the Kansas plains during the heyday of the cattle drives, or of the gangs that followed them would fill a book in itself. But this will summarize the highlights of one of the cowboys born to be bad.

Charlie Coulter was one of those people who could be an angel when sober or a devil when drunk. Coulter's problem was that he was drunk about as much time as he was sober. He was a hard worker and a knowledgeable employee.

Coulter went on his first cattle drive when he was fifteen. He was originally from Missouri and when he was grown, he stood an inch over six feet tall and weighed two hundred pounds. That weight was all muscle and any man who challenged him, whether with fists or guns, usually regretted it – if he lived that long.

Coulter was the fourth member of his family to die with his boots on. The one male member still alive had consumption and would surely miss the distinction that marked the passing of each of his brothers.

Charlie spent most of his life working cattle except for a couple of years when he took a turn with the James-Younger gang. He didn't like robbing stage coaches and railroad trains so he went back to cattle.

He thoroughly enjoyed a good fight. In one fight in Dodge City, he went up against

Main Street of Leotia,
Kansas in the 1880s

Kansas State Historical Society

Main Street of Leoti as
it looks today.

Author's photo

thirteen men, the newspaper reported, and came out alive. It was a landmark battle. Twelve men were either killed or seriously wounded.

He wasn't much for running from a fight. But after that debacle in Dodge City, several of the friends of the wounded and dead men set out to settle the score with Coulter. They failed to find him. He had wisely disappeared..

After that squabble, he settled down for a year. But then he got riled and, according to the papers, he and four companions "rounded up" the town of Wallace, near the Colorado line, and held it captive for two days.

During the Wallace episode, he got a meal in a small restaurant. There was a cus-tomer there eating milk toast because his stomach demanded it. Coulter called that dish "graveyard stew." He made the man stand up against the wall and he outlined his figure with bullet holes, grazing him a time or two but never injuring him.

Then he got into the battle at Coronado. The Coulter luck ran out. The men of Coronado ruled the day. But even with fourteen bullets in him, Charlie managed to empty both his guns before he collapsed.

Author's photo

The site of old Coronado. The town has disappeared

Ambush at Coronado
Wichita County — February, 1892

The participants argued that the fight in the streets of Coronado, Kansas that Sunday evening in February, 1892, had nothing to do with the battle for the county seat. Few people believed that.

Coronado and Leotia (Leoti) were only three miles apart and were the two largest towns in the new county. On that Kansas prairie, the residents of the two towns were so close together they could almost spy on each other. In a country of such sparse population, it was obvious that the winner of the county seat would be the biggest town in the county and the loser would disappear. There simply weren't enough people and probably never would be, for two towns to survive that close together.

There were hard feelings between the towns, but there were also people in both communities who were friendly with each other.

On that particular Sunday, the weather was warm enough to encourage a group from Leotia to make the three-mile trip to Coronado to see their friends. The group included Charlie Coulter, who had become a druggist; Raines, a liveryman; Johnson, a real estate agent; Beerey, a lumber merchant; Denning, a farmer; and two other young men, Watkins and Jenners.

They packed all seven in a two-seated buggy and made the short drive across the prairie. In Coronado, they met their friends in a drug store and had some drinks. After a good afternoon, the Leotia boys got in their buggy (some versions say it was a wagon and, since there were seven men in it, that may be correct) and started home.

At the main corner, where the east-west road split the town, the Leotia boys turned their team to the west on the road home. There were three or four Coronado boys on the sidewalk at the corner. One of them threw a challenge at the Leotia boys, yelling that he could whip any so-and-so from Leotia.

Three of the Leotia representatives leaped out of the buggy, led by Coulter. It was a well known fact that Coulter could be a wild man when he was drunk. And he had been imbibing that afternoon.

The three charged toward the Coronado boys. That was when the guns opened up. The shots came from the billiard hall, the post office building, the rooms above the bank on the corner, and from the upper story of the building across the street. The Leotia boys were caught in a deadly crossfire.

It was estimated that more than a hundred shots were fired in a matter of minutes. Coulter was killed with fourteen bullets in his body. Raines was also killed. Watkins was severely wounded and died the next day.

The horses, although wounded, were whipped into a run to the west and home. Beerey, badly wounded, was on the floor. Denny was shot in the shoulder, Jenners was shot twice in the back.

All the wounded got back to Leotia. The buggy (or wagon) had over sixty bullet holes in it. It apparently had been a well planned ambush.

The story that reached the papers was that Coulter and Raines had been in Coronado a few weeks before and had almost precipitated a confrontation then. It had finally culminated in the ambush that killed three and wounded four more.

Yet when the courts called up the men believed to have masterminded the ambush, not one of them would admit that he even knew anything about the plans until the shooting started.

Author's photo

Main Street of Sharon Springs, Kansas
as it looks today.

Doolin Gang Train Robbery Gray County — June 11, 1893

The area around Dodge City and Cimarron refused to calm down and act civilized. Cimarron was the scene of another outlaw raid just four years after the county seat war with Ingalls. This time it was an attempted train robbery.

It was shortly after midnight on a warm June night in 1893 that Bill Doolin and his gang struck at the Southern California and New Mexico Express on the Santa Fe line. They made their plans carefully, stopping the train just a half mile west of Cimarron before the it got up speed. They did that by throwing up the danger sign along the track.

The engineer obeyed the sign and stopped the train. Doolin put his gun on the engineer and forced him to get off the engine. Then he marched him back along the line of cars to the Wells Fargo car.

Doolin knew there was $10,000 in the safe in the express car. He forced the engineer to batter down the door with a sledge hammer. But there his luck ran out.

There were two safes in the car. One was for local use and contained only small amounts of money and valuables going just a short distance. The other was the big safe that was going through to a pre-determined station. It had a time lock on it so that it couldn't be opened before it reached its destination. The $10,000 was in that safe.

Doolin was stymied. They were too close to Cimarron to stall long enough to find some way to blast open the safe. Someone in town would notice that the train was stopped when it should be moving away toward the next station.

Doolin could force the guard to open the local safe. So he did and got nearly a thousand dollars out of that. Then the gang had to ride fast to get out of reach of the law.

They went southeast past Ashland into Oklahoma. There they were caught by the law. Bill Doolin was stopped by a bullet in his foot. Running away, even on a horse, was out of the question with a hole in his foot.

Corley Murder
Wallace County — May 3, 1894

It could have been called a family fight or a neighborhood feud or perhaps it was a combination of both. It happened in the rural country about eighteen miles north of Sharon Springs, the county seat of Wallace County. It took place years after the country had supposedly progressed beyond feuds.

The McKinleys had a daughter, Lottie, who fell in love with a neighbor boy, Sprague Corley. The two wanted to get married. The Corleys were in favor of the marriage and Mrs. McKinley agreed. But Mr. McKinley said that his daughter was too young and he didn't like Sprague Corley, anyway. He further alienated his daughter by suggesting that he should at least get a new wagon from Corley. She thought that was the same as selling her.

Sprague Corley and his new bride settled on a farm not far from the homes of their parents. In addition to Lottie, Bill McKinley had two sons, Louis, grown, and Fred, just seventeen. Bill's hatred of Corley spread to his offspring. They agreed that they would get rid of Corley the first chance they got.

The days passed peacefully and spring work got under way. Then came the day when Fred McKinley went to Corley and offered to help him with his farm work. Corley believed it was a move toward reconciliation between him and the McKinleys, so he quickly agreed to hire Fred to help him.

Sprague Corley had a hotbed a ways from the house where he was getting some plants started for his early garden. Lottie had gone to Sharon Springs with one of the McKinleys to get some things.

It was while the men were at the hotbed and Corley was stooped over, working with the plants, that Fred spotted a grubbing hoe near the end of the hotbed. He grabbed it

Kansas State Historical Society

The lynching of William and Louis McKinley

and brought the heavy blade down with a mighty stroke on the top of Corley's head. The blow killed him instantly.

Fred dragged the body to some soft dirt and buried it. From evidence found later, Fred apparently was frightened away before he had completed the job because the body was not completely covered The hands and part of the head were left exposed.

Fred disappeared, taking Corley's gun, horse and saddle. He went to Kit Carson, Colorado and stayed with some people he knew there who owned a sheep ranch.

When Lottie got home from Sharon Springs that evening, Sprague wasn't there. He hadn't come in yet the next morning and she was worried. Mrs. Corley, Sprague's mother, was there and she shared Lottie's worry.

It was Mrs. Corley who found Sprague late in the afternoon. She saw some hogs feeding on something down by the garden and she discovered that they were eating on the head and hands of her dead son. The shock was almost more than she could endure.

Mrs. Corley's screams brought a neighbor, Mr. Paxton, who happened to be passing by. When he saw the situation, he jumped on his horse and rode wildly to a place where he knew several people were having a party. Among those at the party was Sheriff Fleming. The celebration ended abruptly and everyone came back with Mr. Paxton.

The grubbing hoe and the tracks around the body told the story. Everyone, including Sheriff Fleming, knew how Bill McKinley felt about Sprague Corley. They all agreed that Bill McKinley had probably committed the murder.

Bill McKinley and his older son, Louis, had actually been out searching for Sprague Corley. The sheriff immediately placed the two McKinleys under arrest for the murder. They, of course, denied it. The sheriff was convinced that, if they hadn't done the killing themselves, they had hired or coaxed someone to do it.

They were taken to Sharon Springs and put in the jail there. A man was put on the trail of young Fred since he was missing and could be involved.

The deputy found Fred McKinley down in Colorado and brought him back to Sharon Springs and lodged him, under guard, in the hotel.

Feelings ran very high among the people, especially the friends of Corley. A grizzly murder of a friend couldn't be tolerated. No one seemed particularly concerned about the positive identity of the actual killer. They were absolutely sure that Bill McKinley and his son were behind the murder, regardless of who had swung the grubbing hoe.

It was an impromptu mob. They had seen with their own eyes what had happened to Sprague Corley. They could not wait for the slow grinding wheels of the law to determine the fate of the McKinleys. So they dragged McKinley and his son, Louis, out of the Sharon Springs jail and down to the railroad bridge at the southwest corner of town. They lynched them both in spite of their pleas that they were not guilty of killing Sprague Corley.

Fred McKinley asked for a change of venue for his trial. Feeling was far too high in Wallace County for him to get a fair trial. So his trial was moved to Wakeeney. There, to the surprise of many people, Fred McKinley was found not guilty.

The Ballad of the Berry Boys

Way out on the plains of Kansas
Where the wind blows hard and hot,
Stands a little old sod shanty
Where the Berry boys were shot.

Two men in the prime of manhood –
And a man with silvery hair
Were cruelly murdered that bright day
By the outlaw millionaire.

Must wives be changed to widows
In the space of a fleeting breath
And the children be made orphans
And men be shot to death?

It is hard to believe it true
In this land we love so well
It is hard for us to believe
That men will their honor sell.

Oh, is there no punishment
For this murderer's blood-stained hand?
Is there no court of justice
In this glorious Christian land?

I would think the murderers,
Although they may be free,
Those quiet and deathly faces
In troubled dreams would see.

That aged and furrowed brow
Those blood-stained locks of gray—
I think that Chauncey Dewey
Would see them night and day.

The jury has cleared the savages,
The court its verdict has given
But they'll find when through this life
They can't buy the courts of heaven!

Page 112

VI
1900 — 1910

Turn of the Century Bad Men

Death to Train Robbers
Sherman County —
August 10, 1900

The days of robbing stage coaches had rolled into history. But men who wanted to steal found other targets. The dawning of the twentieth century didn't blot out the crimes or the criminals of the nineteenth century.

It was barely past the midnight hour, August 5, 1900, when two men who had boarded the train at Limon, Colorado, entered a Pullman car. With guns drawn, they moved quietly down the aisle, forcing the conductor to nudge each passenger awake and then, placing a gun in the sleepy man's face, demanding his money and jewelry.

The two men moved to the other Pullman car and repeated the process. Only one man failed to obey their orders. When told to give up his money, William J. Fay, manager of the Pintsch Gas Company of Los Angeles, pulled a small pistol and fired it at the men. He missed but both robbers fired back. One bullet struck Fay in the mouth and came out the back of his head. That made the duo murderers as well as robbers.

High Plains Museum, Goodland, Kansas

Sherman County Sheriff William Walker, left, and Deputy Sheriff George Cullins.

At Hugo, about fifteen miles southeast of Limon, the two robbers jumped off the train. The robbery and murder were reported by the conductor. But it was night and no one knew which way the men had gone.

The robbers went where the railroad detectives wouldn't expect them to go. They angled to the northeast and caught an eastbound train out of Flagler on a different railroad line.

They rode the train to Goodland, Kansas and searched for a place to stay. They were not going to remain in town where people would see them. They inquired at several houses before they found a family willing to board them. They finally found what they were looking for at the rural home of D. E. Bartholomew.

For a few days, the hiding place worked well for the outlaws. Every day the men sent the Bartholomew boy into Goodland to get the latest *Denver Post* so they could keep up on the news of the search for the train robbers.

The robbery occurred about 1 A.M., Sunday morning, August 5. It was Thursday, August 9, before anyone got suspicious of the boarders at Bartholomew's farm.

William Hogeboom told Sheriff William Walker that his daughter-in-law had visited the Bartholomews and there were two men staying there who she thought looked suspicious. The railroad had sent descriptions of the two robbers to every town in every direction from the place where the men had left the train, including Goodland.

The sheriff was eager to get a look at the two strangers and planned to raid the place that night. But his wife begged him to wait until morning when he could take a posse with him.

Early on Friday morning, August 10, the sheriff organized his posse. But he feared

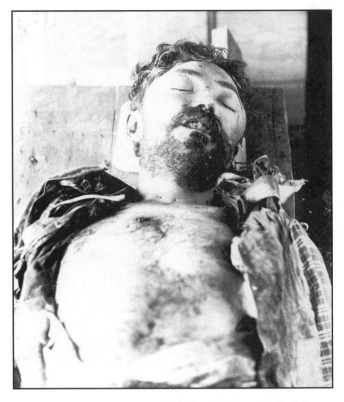

High Plains Museum, Goodland, Kansas
Body of one of the two Jones brothers, killed by
Sheriff Walker and his posse.

the daylight approach would be more dangerous than his previous plan.

He planned his move carefully. He swore in six deputies. John Riggs and George Cullins rode horses as did the sheriff. The other four, C. E. Biddison, G. M. Phillips, and C. S. Cox, rode in William Hogeboom's surrey.

The sheriff borrowed some horses and they drove them into the Bartholomew yard, ostensibly to get water. The sheriff hoped the ruse would bring the robbers out of the house. But it brought them only to the doors.

The house was in two parts. The west section was a low roofed sod house while the east part was a two story frame building. The wanted men were staying in the sod half of the house. But they didn't come out to investigate like normal boarders. The soddy had a south door and a west door. One man went to each door and watched the newcomers.

The Bartholomew family came out to talk to the sheriff but the robbers stayed inside. The sheriff 's ruse didn't work. If the men wouldn't come out, the posse would have to go in.

With guns drawn, the sheriff and his two deputies ran forward. The robbers ducked back inside the house. When the lawmen rushed inside, guns popped. Soon the interior of the house was filled with powder smoke.

William Hogeboom whipped his team into a run when he saw what was happening at the house. The sheriff and his deputies dodged out of the house since they couldn't see anything inside. Both robbers charged outside, still shooting. Deputy Riggs was hit and put out of the fight. Cullins was also hit but not wounded as seriously as Riggs.

One of the robbers was hit and he fell. But he leaped up and ran across the yard. Biddison, who was out of the surrey now, leveled his Winchester and shot the robber, the bullet hitting him in the head. The dead bandit's partner dashed back inside the house, going across into the two story frame section. There he got a rifle and, from an upstairs window, began shooting at the posse. Hurriedly, the lawmen retreated out of sight of the window.

There were a lot of shots fired into the house but none seemed to hit the right spot. Rifle shots kept coming from the dwelling. While the fight continued, the attackers put the wounded posse members in the surrey and drove them into Goodland where a doctor could care for them.

Some men, impatient at the impasse, decided to set the house on fire and smoke out their quarry. People from town swarmed out to get in the fight. But the excitement was about all they could share. The rifleman inside was careful to keep out of sight except to occasionally shoot into the yard.

Somebody brought some railroad fuses and two men volunteered to sneak in and use them to set the house on fire. With guns all around the house, it was impossible for the penned up robber to watch all sides at once.

With everyone who had a gun firing at the house, the two ran for the house, keeping low. No shots came their way.

Once close to the house and out of line from the window, they lit the fuses and threw them on the roof, then dashed back to a safe distance. The fuses ignited the dry shingles and the house started to burn. The posse waited for the robber to dash outside but he didn't appear.

Eventually, the whole house was ablaze and the ammunition inside began to explode like popcorn in a hot skillet. The posse knew then that the man was not going to come out.

The next day they found the burned remains of the robber in the ashes of the building. They put them with the dead robber who was killed in the yard and buried them together in a common grave in the Goodland cemetery.

A week later, the bodies were exhumed for examination by railroad officials and men from Springfield, Missouri. They were able to identify the unburned corpse as one of the Jones brothers, James and Tom, of Springfield. They had a long record of robberies and murders. The burned remains were assumed to be those of the other brother.

The two posse members who were wounded recovered. The Union Pacific Railroad gave an award to Sheriff Walker and the two wounded deputies, John Riggs and George Cullins. The Bartholomew family was given eleven hundred dollars, a price they agreed would rebuild their house.

The Dewey-Berry War
Cheyenne County — June 3, 1903

Many range wars of the 1870s and 1880s went into the history books as battles between cattle and sheep raisers; ranchers versus homesteaders; and often between big ranchers and little ranchers trying to get big. Many were bloody and often settled nothing. Most range wars were history by the turn of the century.

But not in northwestern Kansas in 1903. If the Dewey-Berry fight had to be classified, it would fall in the rancher-homesteader category.

The story starts with Chauncey Dewey, a young man born "with a silver spoon in his mouth." His father, C. P. Dewey, had made plenty of money in Chicago and was also a very shrewd opportunist. When the drought of the early 1890s struck the Plains, few homesteaders could pay their taxes. C. P. Dewey paid those delinquent taxes on land that he didn't own. According to the law, if the land owners didn't pay the taxes, then the person who had paid them owned the land. C. P. Dewey took over many homesteads.

When Chauncey Dewey, the son, was ready to take command of some project, his father handed him the management of the 11,000-acre spread that he had built during the previous ten years. It was all connected, mostly in Cheyenne County. But parts of it spilled over into Rawlins County on the east, Sherman County on the south, and Thomas County to the southeast. It covered more than seventeen square miles. Being

Kansas State Historical Society
Chauncey Dewey

manager of that much land and everything on it was a heady experience for a young man in his early twenties.

There were many disgruntled neighbors around the big ranch. Many of them were former homesteaders who had lost their land to C. P. Dewey. There also were some squatters who had never owned any of the land but, by twisted reasoning, felt entitled to some small share of it, anyway.

Young Chauncey Dewey faced a bigger challenge than his father anticipated. The elder Dewey always managed to get what he wanted and he expected his son to hold

Re-enactment of the
Dewey-Berry feud

*Thomas County Museum,
Colby, Kansas*

what he had and take more if the opportunity presented itself.

Chauncey Dewey had particular trouble with Daniel Berry and his three sons, Alphaeus, Burchard, and Beach, and their cousin, Roy. They had been squatting on Dewey land for several years and C. P. Dewey hadn't put them off. They felt they had a right to the land and resented being "shoved around."

The Berrys held an auction on June 2, 1903. Some of the people from the LV Ranch, Dewey's brand, attended the sale and bought a big wooden tank. Chauncey had a place for the tank nearer the LV headquarters. The men who bid on the tank for Chauncey tried to take it home after the sale. But the Berrys ran them off. They apparently couldn't bear to see the Deweys get something that they once owned.

The day after the sale, June 3, Chauncey took eight of his cowboys with him to get the tank. They were on their own land but the Berrys were staying in the nearby house.

Chauncey knew the Berrys might cause trouble when his men loaded the tank, so he and his hands were all armed. He sent one

man to the house to tell Daniel Berry that they had come for the tank.

Daniel Berry and his oldest son, Alphaeus, came down from the house and were talking to the Dewey men when the other two sons, Burchard and Beach, along with their cousin, Roy, rode up

Up to that point, there had been no trouble. According to Chauncey, Daniel Berry had given permission for the men to load up the tank. They were draining it when Daniel Berry and his son arrived.

There was disagreement over who fired the first shot. Each side said it was the other. But years later, the surviving Berrys admitted they fired first. They claimed they fired over the heads of the Deweys in an attempt to scare them away. If so, that would explain how the Deweys escaped harm. And it would verify the Deweys' charge that the Berrys fired first and they just reacted to those shots.

The Berrys did not fare well in the fight. Daniel Berry, the father, and sons, Alphaeus and Burchard, were killed. Beach Berry and his cousin, Roy, were wounded. None of the Deweys suffered any wounds. Three of their horses were killed, which doesn't say much for the marksmanship of the Berrys.

The wounded Berrys filed a charge of murder and the sheriff of Thomas County arrested Chauncey Dewey and two of his hands, Clyde Wilson and W. J. McBride. They were taken to jail in Colby, although the shooting took place just over the line in Cheyenne County.

There was a concerted public outcry against the rich rancher who had everything and had killed those who were trying to make an honest living. It was interpreted as a warning to other homesteaders to get out of the way of the Deweys, who planned to take over the whole country.

The sentiment was against the Deweys. The feeling of the homesteaders was so strong because, in their opinion, C. P. Dewey had virtually stolen the land from the rightful owners by paying the back taxes.

Because the fight took place in Cheyenne County, the prisoners had to face the charges in the Cheyenne County Court in St. Francis.

The sheriff of Cheyenne County came to Colby to escort the prisoners to St. Francis. Lynch talk was rampant around the area. The sheriff brought along twenty-five armed men to guard the prisoners on their trip of almost fifty miles across the open prairie to St. Francis.

Someone reported that there were a 135 armed men at the Berry place waiting until the prisoners started to St. Francis. A huge necktie party was being planned for the Deweys.

The trip was delayed until a company of National Guard troops arrived to go with the procession to St. Francis. That many armed men apparently discouraged the lynch party and they made no effort to intercept the prisoners.

But the feeling against the LV ranchers did not subside. They might have to wait for the trial to see that justice was done. To fan the hatred that was already seething in those who resented the rich men, Berry opponents re-enacted the battle scene and took pictures of the dead and dying. They put the pictures on the new invention that was becoming popular, the magic lantern.

The Kansas Supreme Court ruled the prisoners could be released on bond. A change of venue sent the trial to Norton, Kansas, where it began on February 7, 1904.

The surviving Berrys, made a strong case, swearing they never carried arms and were unarmed when they were shot down. That, they said, was why none of the Deweys were injured.

The key witness for the defense was a representative of a Nebraska threshing machine company. He said he had gone to the Berry farm to pick up some horses that had been listed as security for some machinery the Berrys had bought and not paid for. The Berrys shot at him and chased him away. He refuted their claim that they always went unarmed.

After some deliberation, the jury brought in its verdict. Chauncey Dewey, Clyde Wilson and W. J. McBride were not guilty of the murder of any of the Berrys.

The jury's decision wasn't popular with the homesteaders. Someone even wrote a poem that was published in several area newspapers.

The Ballad of the Berry Boys

Way out on the plains of Kansas
Where the wind blows hard and hot,
Stands a little old sod shanty
Where the Berry boys were shot.

Two men in the prime of manhood –
And a man with silvery hair
Were cruelly murdered that bright day
By the outlaw millionaire.

Must wives be changed to widows
In the space of a fleeting breath
And the children be made orphans
And men be shot to death?

It is hard to believe it true
In this land we love so well
It is hard for us to believe
That men will their honor sell.

Oh, is there no punishment
For this murderer's blood-stained hand?
Is there no court of justice
In this glorious Christian land?

I would think the murderers,
Although they may be free,
Those quiet and deathly faces
In troubled dreams would see.

That aged and furrowed brow
Those blood-stained locks of gray—
I think that Chauncey Dewey
Would see them night and day.

The jury has cleared the savages,
The court its verdict has given
But they'll find when through this life
They can't buy the courts of heaven!

Many insisted the verdict was wrong. That feeling prevailed through the decades until 1934 when Beach and Roy Berry signed affidavits stating they had fired first that day, aiming to scare the Deweys away. They also said they made false statements to the court at the suggestion of their attorney. They said all firearms were removed from the scene before the sheriff and coroner's jury arrived.

Kersenbrock Murder
Thomas County — 1905

Henry Kersenbrock was a huge man. Some said he was as strong as a bull. He came to Colby, Kansas on a cold day in January, 1905, to attend the trial of August Roupetz, who was charged with assault and battery. Roupetz had reportedly beaten a neighbor girl with a buggy whip when he found her running cattle on his property.

The feeling of the community was very strong against Roupetz. Because the victim was a girl, the fury was greater than if he had whipped a man.

It was not the first time Roupetz had been in trouble with the law. He had a reputation of being quarrelsome and very "touchy." It was easy to get him stirred up.

Kersenbrock had no intention of stirring up Roupetz when he left the courthouse that day. The trial had been delayed because the defense attorney needed more time for preparation. Kersenbrock went to the livery barn and harnessed his team and hitched up. Then he drove to the Colby Mercantile and was going inside for some things he needed when he was stopped by August Roupetz and his brother, Fred.

August was agitated. "Henry," he said, "I hear you said at the trial today that Fred and I both should get the rope. Is that right?"

"I don't remember whether I said that or not," Kersenbrock said. "What do you think about it?"

"If we should have the rope, then so should you!" Roupetz said angrily.

Kersenbrock was not one to take talk like that. He had been a rancher for a long time and was well known in Colby.

"My advice to you," he told Roupetz, "is to go on down the street or I'll have to thrash you."

"You thrash us and you'll never thrash anybody else," Roupetz threatened.

Roupetz lunged at Kersenbrock and the fight was on. Kersenbrock had on a heavy coat against the cold and it fit so tightly over his huge bulk that he was handicapped in maneuvering. Still Kersenbrock was driving Roupetz backward. his strength was far too much for the smaller man.

August Roupetz retreated and fumbled inside his coat as he backed up. Then he pulled out a revolver and fired four shots in rapid succession.

Only one bullet took effect but it went through Kersenbrock's neck and cut the spinal cord. He died almost instantly.

The last murder in Colby had been twenty years earlier in 1885. Deputy Sheriff Suter arrived on the scene quickly, attracted by the shots. August Roupetz was still there and the deputy arrested him and took him to the jail.

Even though it was the twentieth century, there was lynch talk floating around. Kersenbrock belonged back in the nineteenth century and some thought that his killer should receive the penalty that many had received for the crime back in those days. But cool heads prevailed and the town waited for the trial.

Sheriff Sam Pratt arranged for the trial to be held in the old opera house just north of the Commercial Hotel. Selecting a jury from local people who had no opinion about the case proved to be a difficult job. They started with a field of one hundred and sixty people and finally got twelve that both lawyers would accept.

The prosecution tried to establish premeditated murder, saying that Roupetz had come to town armed, looking for an excuse to kill Kersenbrock. The defense pointed out that Kersenbrock was a big burly man, capable of whipping two men the size of Roupetz and when he came charging at Roupetz, the little man had to shoot in self-defense.

The jury was out three days. The first vote was five for murder in the first degree, six in favor of murder in the second degree, and one for acquittal. The final compromise that received all twelve votes was manslaughter.

August Roupetz was sentenced to a maximum of twenty-five years in prison. He served only seven years because he died in 1912.

VII
1910 — 1925

New Century Bad Men

First Topeka Policeman Killed
Shawnee County — May 5, 1912

There weren't many policemen in Topeka in 1912 and they had very little training for their work. Wearing a policeman's badge in Topeka was a political appointment, handed out by the mayor. There were no career policemen.

Caswell Matthews was the first letter carrier in North Topeka. After completing his route each day, he worked in the North Topeka postal station. Then he was appointed to the position of policeman.

He was assigned to watch the railroad station. On May 12, 1912, he was watching especially for two men, Lewis Lagrande and Frank Miller, in connection with the hold-up of the city marshal in Bonner Springs a few days earlier.

He saw two men who seemed to match the descriptions of the fugitives. He moved over and intercepted them and asked several questions which they answered rather evasively.

Matthews was more suspicious and he began to search the two for hidden weapons. It was at that moment that the two pulled their guns and began firing.

One shot hit Matthews in the neck but it

Kansas State Historical Society
Kansas Avenue in early Topeka

didn't keep him from returning the fire. His shot hit Lagrande in the left wrist. The other man, Miller, fired, hitting Matthews in the lung, putting him out of the fight.

Both men fled. Citizens came running to Matthews and they carried him to a home where he died the next day. Pursuit of the killers was prompt and they were captured much quicker than most had expected.

Less than two days after they shot Matthews, the two killers were convicted of murder and sentenced to life in prison. Even then, a life sentence didn't mean what it said. Lewis Lagrande was released from prison in October, 1923, eleven years after killing Matthews. Frank Miller was released in May, 1929, exactly seventeen years after the killing.

Sheriff Sam Pratt Killed
Thomas County —
September 24, 1925

Sam Pratt was an early settler in western Kansas. He freighted in the 1880s. To keep from starving in the drought of the 1890s, he worked on Cheyenne Mountain at Colorado Springs, building a lake for the water supply for the city. He also worked on the cog railroad to the top of Pike's Peak.

But Pratt spent most of his life near Colby. In 1902, he was elected sheriff of Thomas County and was elected again in 1904. After a gap, he was elected in 1910 and again in 1922. He was re-elected for the last time in 1924. It was during this term that he answered a call that cost him his life.

The sheriff got a report from North Platte, Nebraska, to be on the lookout for two robbers who had killed a policeman in that city and stolen a Buick car.

Pratt got together a posse of six men and went to a place on the highway called Wisdom Bridge. If the robbers didn't switch to another highway, they would almost certainly come down that road. There weren't many good roads through the country at that time.

They blocked the road with an old truck sitting crossways on the grade. About midnight the Buick came roaring over the hill and down to the bridge. The driver slammed on the brakes and stopped the car just short of a collision with the truck then threw the car into reverse and wheeled around. The car slipped off the grade in making the turn.

Sheriff chose that moment to order the men to get out of the car. One of the robbers shot the sheriff in the heart.

The driver slammed the car into gear and back on the road then roared up the hill, going back the way they had come. The

Thomas County Museum, Colby, Kansas

Thomas County Sheriff Sam Pratt

others in the posse fired at the Buick but it kept going.

It was a sad day for Colby when one of its most popular men was brought back for burial.

The robbers were finally apprehended a long way to the south. One was killed and the other taken back to Nebraska for trial. He was convicted and sent to prison.

A Deserved Lynching
Rawlings County —
April 18, 1932

This quick glance at the deadly days in Kansas was scheduled to stop in the early twentieth century. But a story from the 1930s proved the public attitudes that led to shootings and lynchings in the early days had not completely died out when the first quarter of the twentieth century became history.

Dorothy Hunter attended school in the little town of Selden, Kansas. Eight years old on March 11, she was in the second grade. She started home after school on April 15. But she discovered she had forgotten her lunch bucket and hurried back to the school to get it.

Coming back out to the street, she was far behind her companions so she hurried to catch up. That was when the Model A Ford car slowed and the driver invited her to get in and ride.

The Hunters waited for their daughter to come home. Her nine-year-old sister, Alice, came home, as did her six-year-old brother, Doyle. She also had a brother, Dale, age four. But that evening, the Hunters had one child missing.

Dorothy's parents notified the sheriff and search parties were organized. They combed the town and the nearby countryside. When they didn't find Dorothy, alarm spread.

On Friday, intensive searching continued. They knew Dorothy wasn't in town and worry became a premonition of disaster. They sent out descriptions of the girl on the local radio station. She was about four and half feet tall, weighed about fifty pounds, and had brown eyes and auburn hair. Listeners were advised that if anyone saw a girl answering that description, they should notify police immediately. No one responded.

The sheriff of Logan County, Ernest Beaver, became interested in the case. He turned up evidence that indicated the girl might have been kidnapped by Richard Read, a fifty-three-year-old farmer from Rexford, the town just to the southwest of Selden.

Among bits of evidence that pointed to Read was that he had served six years in the Colorado penitentiary in Canon City for assaulting a fifteen-year-old girl in

Thomas County Museum, Colby, Kansas
Sheriff E. H. McGinley, left, and prisoner Rich Read.

Burlington, Colorado.

The sheriff knew that Read had a Model A Ford. One man said he saw a Model A Ford with a man and a small girl Thursday evening north of town. Another man named Anderson reported he saw a car parked south of his place about eleven miles northwest of town around six o'clock.

Investigators discovered the suspicious car had tires with a peculiar tread. Searchers found the tread marks in many places — as if the car had been driven here and there around the country.

The sheriff went to the Read farm where Rich Read, a bachelor, still lived with his parents. There was a Model A Ford there with the same tread they had noticed in so many places. Rich Read was taken into custody.

His story was that he had been kidnapped by four well dressed strangers who kept him all night and took him far up into Nebraska.

But some carefully worded grilling brought out the truth. Rich Read admitted that he kidnapped Dorothy Hunter near the Selden schoolhouse on Thursday evening and later murdered her.

Read was taken to the Thomas County Jail in Colby. But a mob soon gathered and the sheriff could stall the furious people only by telling them he had to keep Read alive to tell where the girl's body was buried.

On Saturday, Read told the law officers that he had buried the body in a small stack in a wheat field. He said he could take them to the spot.

They took him to the roads that he said he had traveled. He remembered he had gone through a gate into a field. After some searching, they found a gate leading into a wheat field. They found the body of Dorothy Hunter in a small stack of hay. It showed signs of severe abuse. Read said he and the girl had eaten breakfast Friday morning at Atwood and he had killed her about 10 o'clock.

Sheriff McGinley of Thomas County took charge of Read and spirited him away from the furious people who were determined to make him pay for his deed.

The people of Selden in particular were caught up in mob fever and they had plenty of encouragement from surrounding towns. That Sheriff McGinley kept Read out of their hands is little short of a miracle.

Sunday was a quieter day for the sheriff. Dorothy Hunter's funeral was that afternoon. But as soon as it was over, the lynch talk became a crescendo.

Rumors raced through the people as to where Read was being held. Then someone who spoke with authority said he was in the Cheyenne County Jail in St. Francis, quite a distance from the scene of the murder.

After dark Sunday night, a string of cars headed for St. Francis, their lights forming a parade a mile long. In St. Francis, they searched for Sheriff Bacon and found him at a filling station. Under threat of death, they forced him to turn over the keys to the jail.

In the jail, they found Read on a cot on the third floor. They quickly tied a rope around his neck and led him from the building to a waiting car. That car led the parade out of St. Francis and east through Bird City into Rawlins County, where the murder took place. The long line of cars went through McDonald and then to the southeast to a valley where there were some cottonwood trees.

They led Read under one of the trees, tossed the end of the rope over a stout limb and then paused to ask him if he would admit that he killed Dorothy Hunter.

Reluctantly, Read nodded. He said he wouldn't have done it if he hadn't been drunk. Few doubted that statement but it didn't change any minds about the punishment he deserved.

Several men were holding the end of the rope. One stood with one arm raised. Suddenly he dropped his arm and strong hands jerked on the rope. Read was left hanging with his feet a full yard from the ground.

The crowd stayed at the scene for twenty minutes. There was a tone of satisfaction in their voices as they quietly discussed what had happened. Then, one-by-one, the cars headed home.

Most members of the mob agreed that it was a job that had to be done. Colorado had sent Read to prison for exactly the same crime. It hadn't saved Dorothy Hunter's life. The people of Kansas were determined not to repeat Colorado's mistake.

ACKNOWLEDGMENTS

It often takes many helping hands to convert an idea into a tangible fact. Many of those helping hands reached out to me as I put together some of the stories that gives a glimpse of the struggles that the early settlers fought through to bring into being the peaceful state of Kansas that we know today.

As she has done in so many of my previous research assignments, Elinor Brown, librarian of the Imperial Public Library in Imperial, Nebraska, found books and magazines that were a great help to me in seeking out details of the stories I needed.

The Kansas State Historical Society library directed me to rolls of microfilm of newspapers that yielded many stories. At the Archives Division, Nancy Sherbert, curator of photographs, and her helpers brought out many packages of pictures from which I could choose the ones that would illustrate the stories.

Dorothy Janke and Marge Wright, historians of Russell Springs, Kansas, found stories and pictures that I couldn't find elsewhere and my thanks goes to them for some stories and pictures that could only have come from their files.

The crew at the Thomas County Historical Society museum, Colby, Kansas--- Janice Linville, Kelly Hibbs, Judy Kleinsorge, and Sue Taylor – dug up stories and pictures that I had failed to find elsewhere.

The same can be said of Tina Goodwin, director of the High Plains Museum at Goodland, Kansas. And Opal Loomis and Rosetta Lindsten of the Goodland Public Library came up wih some very helpul stories.

My good friend, Bob Chew of Atchison, Kansas, furnished me with the newspaper story and picture of his great-grandfather, Lew Chew, an Atchison policeman in the late 1870s who was killed in the line of duty.

My sincere thanks goes to the historians of Medicine Lodge, Kansas, particularly John W. Nixon, vice president of the First National Bank, who loaned me the negatives of pictures that were very important to the book, and to Rosalee Armstrong, Librarian, and her helpers at the Lincoln Library in Medicine Lodge for the newspaper story of the bank robbery, murder, and lynching that shocked the town in the late nineteenth century.

My thanks to the many others who helped me with pictures and stories, particularly Loral Johnson, publisher of the *Imperial Republican*, Imperial, Nebraska, who dug up a picture I had been unable to find elsewhere.

Without help like this, the book could never have been completed and my thanks goes out to each and every one.

BIBLIOGRAPHY

BOOKS

Blue, Daniel. *Thrilling Narrative of the Adventures, Sufferings and Starvations of Pike's Peak Gold Seekers of the Plains of the West in the Winter and Spring of 1859.* Chicago: Evening Journal Steam Print, 1860. Reprint, Fairfield, WA: Ye Galleon Press, 1968

Campbell, C. E. *Down Among the Red Men,* Kansas Historical Collections 1926-1928 17 (1928)

Connelley, William Elsey, Edited by. *Collections of the Kansas State Historical Society, 1926-1928,* Vol. XVII. Topeka, KS: 1928

Dary, David. *True Tales of Old Time Kansas.* New York: Crown Publishers, 1979. Reprint. Topeka, KS: University Press of Kansas, 1984

Duffus, R. L. *The Santa Fe Trail.* Albuquerque, NM: University of New Mexico Press, 1930

Editors of *Guns and Ammo. Guns and Gunfighters.* New York: Bonanza Books, 1982

Gardner, Theodore. *An Episode in Kansas History: The Doy Rescue.* Kansas Historical Collections 1926-1928 17 (1928)

Hunt, Frazier. *The Long Trail from Texas.* New York: Doubleday, Doran & Co., 1940

Hunter, J. Marvin, Edited b. *The Trail Drivers of Texas.* San Antonio, TX: Globe Printing Co., 1924

Johnson, Alma D. *Trail Dust Over the B.O.D. Through Kansas.* Detroit. MI: Harlo Press, 1975

Lee. Wayne C. & Raynesford, Howard C. *Trails of the Smoky Hill.* Caldwell, ID: Caxton Printers, Ltd., 1980

Linville, Leslie & Bertha. *Tales of the Smoky Hill.* Colby, KS: Leroy's Printing Company, 1989

Long, Margaret. *The Smoky Hill Trail.* Denver: W. H. Kistler Company, 1946

McBee, John. *Accounts of the Expedition of the Nineteenth Kansas.* Kansas Historical Collections 1926-1928 17 (1928)

Meredith, Grace E. *Girl Captives of the Cheyennes.* Los Angeles: Gem Publishing Co., 1927

Montgomerv, Mrs. Frank C. *Fort Wallace and its Relations to the Frontier.* Kansas Historical Collections, 1926-1928 17 (1928)

Roach. Mrs. S. T. *Memories of Frontier Days in Kansas: Barber County.* Kansas Historical Collections 1926-1928 17 (1928)

Rogers, Vince. *The German Family Massacre.* Roseberg, OR: Rogers

Rosa, Joseph G. *The Gunfighter, Man or Myth.* Norman, OK: University of Oklahoma Press, 1969

Ross, Edith Connelley. *The Bloody Benders.* Kansas Historical Collections 1926-1928 17 (1928)

Sandoz, Mari. *The Cattlemen.* New York: Hastings House, 1958

Sears, General William Henry. *The Paul Reveres of the Lawrence Raid.* Kansas Historical Collections 1926-1928 17 (1928)

Sheridan, Lieutenant General P. H. *Outline Descriptions of the Posts in the Military Division of the Missouri.* Chicago IL: Headquarters Military Division of the Missouri, 1867. Reprint: Bellevue. NE: The Old Army Press, 1969

Smith, Alice Striebe. *Through the Eyes of My Father.* Kansas Historical Collections 1926-1928 17 (1928)

Vestal, Stanley. *Queen of Cowtowns, Dodge City.* New York: Harper & Roe, 1952. Reprint: Lincoln, NE: Bison Books, 1972

Winsor, M. & Scarbrough, James A.. *History of Jewel County, Kansas.* Kansas Historical Collections 1926-1928 17 (1928)

Zornow, William Frank. *Kansas, a History of the Jayhawk State.* Norman, OK: University of Oklahoma Press, 1957

History of Rawlins County, Kansas, Vol. II

MAGAZINES

Dary, David. "The Saga of the Pioneer Sisters." *Kansas City Star Magazine,* December 3, 1972

Davis, Theodore H. "A Stage to Colorado." *Harper's New Monthly Magazine,* July, 1867.

Gray, John S. "Will Comstock, Scout: The Natty Bumpo of Kansas." *Montana Western History* 20, Summer, 1970

Miller, Nyle H. & Richmond, Robert W. "Sheridan, A Fabled End-of-Track Town on the Union Pacific Railroad, 1868-1869." *Kansas Historical Quarterly.* Winter, 1968

Miller, Nyle H. & Snell, Joseph W. "Some Notes on Kansas Towns, Police Officers and Gun Fighters." *Kansas Historical Quarterly,* Spring 1960, Summer 1960, Autumn 1960, Winter 1960

Webb, W. E. "Air Towns and Their Inhabitants." *Harper's New Monthly Magazine,* November, 1875

NEWSPAPERS

Atchison Globe, October 27, 1879

Atchison Weekly Free Press, July 25, 1868; October 26, 1879

The Barber County Index, May 2, 1884

The Coffeeville Journal, October 5, 1892; October 7, 1892

Colby Free Press, August 4, 1925; August 24, 1925

Daily Kansas State Record (Topeka), December 11, 1869

Dodge City Times, August 4, 1877 August 10, 1877; November 10, 1877; April 12, 1878: July 27, 1878; September 28, 1878; October 2, 1878

Ford County Globe, April 8, 1879

Ford County Republican (Dodge City, Kansas) 1892

Kansas City Star, August 9, 1931

Kansas Cowboy, July 20, 1884; September 26, 1884

Kansas Daily Commonwealth, August 22 1871, August 23, 1871, August 27, 1871

Kansas Weekly Tribune (Lawrence), July 30, 1868

Lawrence Daily Tribune, January 24, 1868; September 30, 1869

Lawrence Weekly Tribune, June 18, 1868

Leavenworth Daily Conservative, January 31, 1868

Leavenworth Times, May 8, 1873; May 15, 1875

New York Tribune, December 11, 1969

Thomas County Cat, March 11, 1886

Thomas County Herald, Colby, October 8, 1985

Thomas County Herald (Centennial Edition), 1885-1985

Topeka Commonwealth, August 1, 1869, August 4, 1869

Topeka Daily Capital Journal, November 23, 1958

Topeka State Record, August 26, 1868

The Valley Republican, January 27, 1878; February 9, 1878

Wichita Weekly Beacon, October 2, 1882

INDEX

Other Caxton Books by Wayne C. Lee

Wild Towns of Nebraska
ISBN 0-87004-325-0 147 pages 11 x 8 1/2 paper $14.95

Trails of the Smoky Hill
ISBN 0-87004-276-9 235 pages 11 x 8 1/2 paper $12.95

Bad Men & Bad Towns
ISBN 0-87004-349-8 180 pages 11 x 8 1/2 paper $14.95

Other Caxton Frontier Titles

The Oregon Trail, Yesterday and Today
by William E. Hill
ISBN 0-87004-319-6 179 pages paper $11.95

The Santa Fe Trail, Yesterday and Today
by William E. Hill
ISBN 0-87004-354-4 292 pages paper $12.95

Pioneer Trails West
Western Writers of America
Edited by Donald E. Worcester
ISBN 0-87004-304-8 269 pages cloth $24.95

Plain Enemies: Best True Stories of the Frontier West
by Bob Scott
ISBN 0-87004-364-1 214 pages paper $8.95

Blood at Sand Creek: The Massacre Revisited
by Bob Scott
ISBN 0-87004-361-7 292 pages paper $12.95

For a free catalog of Caxton books write to:

The Caxton Printers, Ltd.
Publishing Department
312 Main Street
Caldwell, ID 83605

or

Visit our Internet Website:

www.caxtonprinters.com